First World War
and Army of Occupation
War Diary
France, Belgium and Germany

51 DIVISION
152 Infantry Brigade
Princess Louise's (Argyll & Sutherland Highlanders)
1/6th Battalion
1 May 1915 - 30 June 1916

WO95/2865/1

The Naval & Military Press Ltd
www.nmarchive.com
Published in association with The National Archives

Published by

The Naval & Military Press Ltd

Unit 10 Ridgewood Industrial Park,

Uckfield, East Sussex,

TN22 5QE England

Tel: +44 (0) 1825 749494

www.naval-military-press.com

www.nmarchive.com

This diary has been reprinted in facsimile from the original. Any imperfections are inevitably reproduced and the quality may fall short of modern type and cartographic standards.

© **Crown Copyright**
Images reproduced by permission of The National Archives, London, England, 2015.

Contents

Document type	Place/Title	Date From	Date To
Heading	WO95/2865 6/Argyll & Sutherland Highlanders May 15-June 16		
Heading	51st Division 152nd Infy Bde 6th Bn A. & S. Hdrs May 1915-Jun 1916		
Heading	51st Division 1/6th A & S. Hd Vol I-31.5.15		
War Diary	Bed Ford	01/05/1915	01/05/1915
War Diary	Folkestone	01/05/1915	01/05/1915
War Diary	Boulogne	02/05/1915	02/05/1915
War Diary	Part De Brique	02/05/1915	02/05/1915
War Diary	Merville	02/05/1915	02/05/1915
War Diary	B Equart Farm (Robecq)	03/05/1915	03/05/1915
War Diary	Wattel Farm (Robecq)	04/05/1915	04/05/1915
War Diary	Lapierre Farm (Robecq)	04/05/1915	14/05/1915
War Diary	Strazeele	15/05/1915	18/05/1915
War Diary	Vielle Chapelle	19/05/1915	20/05/1915
War Diary	La Couture	21/05/1915	28/05/1915
War Diary	Locon	28/05/1915	31/05/1915
Heading	51st Division 1/6th A & S. Hd Vol II 1-30.6.15		
Heading	War Diary Of 1/6th. Battn. Arg. and Suth. Highrs, From 1st June 1915 To 30th June 1915 (Volume IV)		
War Diary	Locon	01/06/1915	05/06/1915
War Diary	Festubert (La Quingue Rue)	06/06/1915	10/06/1915
War Diary	La Couture	10/06/1915	14/06/1915
War Diary	Trenches (La Quinque Rue)	14/06/1915	20/06/1915
War Diary	Le Touret	20/06/1915	22/06/1915
War Diary	Quentin	22/06/1915	24/06/1915
War Diary	Le Touret	24/06/1915	24/06/1915
War Diary	Quentin	25/06/1915	25/06/1915
War Diary	Estaires	26/06/1915	27/06/1915
War Diary	M 6.d.2.0	28/06/1915	30/06/1915
Miscellaneous	152nd. Infantry Brigade 51st. (Highland) Division Hill Corps		
Map	Map		
Miscellaneous	Headquarters 152nd Infantry Brigade	28/06/1915	28/06/1915
Heading	51st Division 1/6th A & S. Hd Vol III 1-31-7-15		
Heading	War Diary Of 1/6th. A. & S. Highrs, From 1st July 1915 To 31st July 1915.		
War Diary	(Sheet 36) M.6.d.2.0.	01/07/1915	09/07/1915
War Diary	La Gorgue	10/07/1915	14/07/1915
War Diary	Laventie	15/07/1915	22/07/1915
War Diary	Vierhouck	23/07/1915	26/07/1915
War Diary	La Houssoye	28/07/1915	30/07/1915
War Diary	Authville	31/07/1915	31/07/1915
Map	Trench Map-Fauquissart-Aubers		
Miscellaneous	Adjt 1/6 And Hrs		
Heading	War Diary Of 1/6th. Battn. Arg. and Suth'd. Highrs. From 1st Aug. 1915 To 31st. Aug. 1915. Vol IV		
War Diary	Authville	01/08/1915	14/08/1915
War Diary	Bresle	14/08/1915	21/08/1915
War Diary	La Boiselle	21/08/1915	31/08/1915

Miscellaneous	War Diary-1/6th. A. & S. Highrs. Appendices		
Map	Plan Directeur 2 B.S		
Map	Map		
Miscellaneous	Appendix II	18/08/1915	18/08/1915
Miscellaneous	Public Record Office		
Miscellaneous	A Form Messages And Signals		
Miscellaneous	51st Division	06/08/1915	06/08/1915
Miscellaneous	Original Document Descriptive Of Trenches Handed Over By Trench At Thiepval		
Heading	51st Division War Diary Of 6th. Battn. Arg. And Suth'd. Highrs. From., 1/9/15 To 30/9/15 (Volume V)		
War Diary	La Boisselle	01/09/1915	01/09/1915
War Diary	Lavieville	02/09/1915	11/09/1915
War Diary	1 Lot (E3) Sector	12/09/1915	17/09/1915
War Diary	Lavieville	18/09/1915	19/09/1915
War Diary	Senlis	20/09/1915	20/09/1915
War Diary	Henencourt	21/09/1915	21/09/1915
War Diary	Aveluy	21/09/1915	26/09/1915
War Diary	Martinsart	27/09/1915	30/09/1915
Miscellaneous	War Diary List of Appendices.	30/09/1915	30/09/1915
Miscellaneous	Public Record Office		
Miscellaneous	51st (Highland) Division. Intelligence Summary.	25/09/1915	25/09/1915
Miscellaneous	51st Division	04/09/1915	04/09/1915
Heading	51st Division. 1/6th Ads. Hrs Vol VI Oct 15		
Heading	War Diary Of 1/6th. Battn. Arg. and Suth'd Highrs. From, 1st. Oct., 1915. To 31st. Oct., 1915. Volume VIII		
War Diary	Thiepval (Sub Sector G.2)	01/10/1915	10/10/1915
War Diary	Martinsart	11/10/1915	20/10/1915
War Diary	Authville	21/10/1915	30/10/1915
War Diary	Millencourt	31/10/1915	31/10/1915
Miscellaneous	List Of Appendices.		
Miscellaneous	Public Record Office		
Miscellaneous	Appendix II 152nd. Infantry Brigade.	14/10/1915	14/10/1915
Miscellaneous	152nd Infantry Brigade 51st Division 10th Corps.	16/10/1915	16/10/1915
Miscellaneous	Public Record Office		
Miscellaneous	Strength Return	02/10/1915	02/10/1915
Miscellaneous	War Diary Of 1/6th. Battalion Argyll and Sutherland Highlanders. From 1st. Nov., 1915. To 30th. Nov. 1915. Vol VII		
War Diary	Millencourt	01/11/1915	07/11/1915
War Diary	Sub Sector F1 (Ovillers)	07/11/1915	14/11/1915
War Diary	Aveluy	14/11/1915	22/11/1915
War Diary	Henencourt	23/11/1915	28/11/1915
War Diary	Thiepval G.2	28/11/1915	30/11/1915
Miscellaneous	Public Record Office		
Miscellaneous	Headquarters 51st. (H) Division.	10/11/1915	10/11/1915
Miscellaneous	Headquarters 51st. (H) Division.	11/11/1915	11/11/1915
Miscellaneous	Headquarters 51st. (H) Division.	12/11/1915	12/11/1915
Miscellaneous	Headquarters 51st. (H) Division.	13/11/1915	13/11/1915
Heading	War Diary Of 1/6th. Argyll & Sutherland Highlanders. From 1st December, 1915. To 31st December, 1915. Vol VIII		
Heading	War Diary Of 1/6th. Battn. Arg. and Suth'd. Highrs. From, 1st. Dec., 1915 To, 31st. Dec., 1915. Volume X.		
War Diary	Thiepval G.2.	01/12/1915	06/12/1915
War Diary	Authville	07/12/1915	11/12/1915

War Diary	Henencourt	11/12/1915	16/12/1915
War Diary	Fl. Sector Ovillers	17/12/1915	19/12/1915
War Diary	Aveluy	20/12/1915	23/12/1915
War Diary	Martinsart	23/12/1915	28/12/1915
War Diary	Beaucourt	28/12/1915	29/12/1915
War Diary	Villers Bocage	29/12/1915	31/12/1915
Heading	1/6th. Battn. Arg. & Suth'd. Highrs. War Diary For January, 1916 Vol IX		
War Diary	Ref. Map Amiens Sheet 12 1/80000 Villers Bocage	01/01/1916	04/01/1916
War Diary	Rubempre	05/01/1916	22/01/1916
War Diary	Acheux	23/01/1916	31/01/1916
Miscellaneous	Appendices For January 1916.		
Miscellaneous	1/6th. Batt, Arg. & Suth'd. Highrs. Training Programme	08/01/1916	08/01/1916
Miscellaneous	1/6th. Batt, Arg. & Suth'd. Highrs. Programme Of Training For Week Ending 22nd January 1916	22/01/1916	22/01/1916
Miscellaneous	Training Programme for Signallers	10/01/1916	10/01/1916
Miscellaneous	Programme Of Training	08/01/1916	08/01/1916
Miscellaneous	Training Programme	22/01/1916	22/01/1916
Heading	War Diary Of 1/6th Bn. Argyll & Sutherland Highlanders. February, 1916. Vol X		
War Diary	Rubempre	01/02/1916	04/02/1916
War Diary	Molliens Au Bois	05/02/1916	09/02/1916
War Diary	Corbie	09/02/1916	29/02/1916
Miscellaneous	Signallers Training Programme	30/01/1916	30/01/1916
Miscellaneous	Scheme For 1st. Feb		
Miscellaneous	Programme Of Training	29/02/1916	29/02/1916
Miscellaneous	Appendix 2	29/02/1916	29/02/1916
Miscellaneous	Programme Of Training	19/02/1916	19/02/1916
Miscellaneous	Scheme For 17th. Feb.	17/02/1916	17/02/1916
Heading	War Diary Of 1/6th Bn. Argyll & Sutherland Highlanders. From 1st March, 1916. To 31st March, 1916. Vol XI		
War Diary	Pierregot	01/03/1916	01/03/1916
War Diary	Rainneville	02/03/1916	05/03/1916
War Diary	Beauval	06/03/1916	09/03/1916
War Diary	Beaudricourt	10/03/1916	10/03/1916
War Diary	Maroeuil	11/03/1916	19/03/1916
War Diary	Labyrinth Sector	20/03/1916	24/03/1916
War Diary	Labyrinth Sector (m.2)	25/03/1916	29/03/1916
War Diary	Sub-Sector M2. (Labyrinth)	30/03/1916	31/03/1916
Miscellaneous	Headquarters, 51st (Highland) Division.	24/03/1916	24/03/1916
Miscellaneous	Headquarters, 51st (Highland) Division.	26/03/1916	26/03/1916
Heading	War Diary Of 1/6th Bn. Arg. & Suth'd. Highlanders. From 1st April, 1916. To 30th April, 1916.		
Heading	War Diary Of 1/6th, Battn. Arg. and Suth'd. Highrs. From 1/4/16 To 30/4/16		
War Diary	Labyrinth Sector	01/04/1916	12/04/1916
War Diary	Maroeuil	12/04/1916	15/04/1916
War Diary	Labyrinth Sector (M.2.)	16/04/1916	21/04/1916
War Diary	Sector M.2.	22/04/1916	22/04/1916
War Diary	Maroeuil	23/04/1916	24/04/1916
War Diary	Ariane	25/04/1916	28/04/1916
War Diary	Ref Trench Map 51b N.W.1 1/10000 A.16.d.	29/04/1916	30/04/1916
Miscellaneous	The Officer Commanding., 1/6th Batt. Arg. & Suthd. Highrs.,	31/03/1916	31/03/1916

Type	Description	Date From	Date To
Miscellaneous	Operation Order No. 4 by Lieut Col R.I. Rawson Commanding 1/6th Battn Arg & Suth'd Highrs	15/04/1916	15/04/1916
Miscellaneous	Operation Order By Captain, N.C. Orr, Commanding 1/6th. Battn. Arg. & Suth'd Highrs.	24/04/1916	24/04/1916
Miscellaneous	1/6th Battn Arg & Suth'd Highrs.	01/05/1915	01/05/1915
Miscellaneous	List Of Officers 1-6th Bn A& S. H.	01/05/1915	01/05/1915
Miscellaneous	1-6th Bn. Arg. & Suth'd Highrs	01/05/1915	01/05/1915
Miscellaneous	1-6th Bn. A & S.H	01/05/1915	01/05/1915
Heading	War Diary Of 1/6th Bn. Argyll and Sutherland Highlanders. From 1st May, 1916. To 31st May, 1916. Vol 13.		
Heading	War Diary Of 1/6th. Bn. Arg. & Suth'd. Highrs. From 1-5-16. To 31-5-16.		
Miscellaneous	152nd Infantry Brigade.	02/06/1916	02/06/1916
War Diary	A.16.d. (Ref. Trench Map 51b. N.W.1, 1/10000	01/05/1916	04/05/1916
War Diary	Ariane	05/05/1916	07/05/1916
War Diary	Maroeuil	08/05/1916	10/05/1916
War Diary	A.16.d. (Ref. Trench Map, 51b, N.W.1. 1/10000)	11/05/1916	17/05/1916
War Diary	Ariane	18/05/1916	23/05/1916
War Diary	Agnieres	24/05/1916	31/05/1916
Miscellaneous	1/6th. Bn. Arg. & Suth'd. Highrs.	31/05/1916	31/05/1916
Miscellaneous	1/6th. Bn. A. & S.H.	30/05/1916	30/05/1916
Miscellaneous	Operation Order By Captain, N.C. Orr, Commanding 1/6th. Battn. Arg. & Suth'd Highrs.	10/05/1916	10/05/1916
Operation(al) Order(s)	Operation Order No. 8. by Lieut Col R.I. Rawson Commanding 1/6th A & Sth	17/05/1916	17/05/1916
Operation(al) Order(s)	Operation Order No. 9. by Lieut Col R.I. Rawson Comdg 1/6th A & Sth	23/05/1916	23/05/1916
Heading	War Diary Of 1/6th. Bn. Arg. & Suth'd. Highrs. From 1-6-16 To 30-6-16.		
War Diary	Agnieres	01/06/1916	02/06/1916
War Diary	Bois Des Alleux	02/06/1916	03/06/1916
War Diary	Ref.51b N.W.1. A.2.b. (Near La Targette)	04/06/1916	09/06/1916
War Diary	Ref 51c. Ecoivres	10/06/1916	12/06/1916
War Diary	Arras	13/06/1916	19/06/1916
War Diary	Lattre	20/06/1916	20/06/1916
War Diary	Grand Rullecourt	21/06/1916	30/06/1916
Heading	1/6th. Battn. Arg. & Suth'd. Highrs. War Diary-June 1916.		
Miscellaneous	Hqrs 51st Division	08/06/1916	08/06/1916
Operation(al) Order(s)	Operation Order No. 11. by Lieut Col R.I. Rawson Commanding 1/6th Bn A & Sh	11/06/1916	11/06/1916
Miscellaneous	Special Order Of The Day By Brig. Gen. W. C. Ross C.B. Comdg 152nd Inf. Brigade.	11/06/1916	11/06/1916
Miscellaneous	1/6th Argyll & Suth'd. Highrs.	11/06/1916	11/06/1916
Operation(al) Order(s)	5th Division Operation Order No. 95	19/06/1916	19/06/1916
Miscellaneous	Table Of Reliefs (Issued With 5th Division Operation Order No. 95)		
Operation(al) Order(s)	95th Inf. Bde. Operation Order No. 128	19/06/1916	19/06/1916
Miscellaneous	Table Of Reliefs 95th Inf. Bde.	19/06/1916	19/06/1916
Miscellaneous	Training Programme	21/06/1916	21/06/1916
Miscellaneous	1/6th. Battn. Arg. & Suth'd. Highrs	22/06/1916	22/06/1916
Miscellaneous	1/6th. Battn. Arg. & Suth'd. Highrs	30/06/1916	30/06/1916
Miscellaneous	List Of Officers 1/6th. Bn. Arg. & Suth'd. Highrs	30/06/1916	30/06/1916

WO 95/2865 ①

6/ Argyll & Sutherland Highlanders

May '15 – June '16

51ST DIVISION
152ND INFY BDE

~~7~~6TH BN A. & S. HDRS
MAY 1915 - JUN 1916

TO 5 DIV (PIONERS)

1.N.

131/5556

15/57° Division

1/6th A&S.H.
Vol I. 1.— 31.5.15.

16th A.I.F. Highrs

WAR DIARY
~~INTELLIGENCE SUMMARY~~
(Erase heading not required.)

Army Form C. 2118.

Instructions regarding War Diaries and Intelligence Summaries are contained in F. S. Regs., Part II. and the Staff Manual respectively. Title pages will be prepared in manuscript.

Place	Date	Hour	Summary of Events and Information	Remarks and references to Appendices
Bedford.	1/5/15	5:25pm	Less Transport & Hqrs. Details. Battalion left for Folkestone in two trains. 1st Train 5:25pm. 2nd Train 5:55pm.	31 officers 987 others
Folkestone	1/5/15	11:30pm	Left for Boulogne in S.S. "Victoria"	
Boulogne	2/5/15	1am	Arrived, disembarked and proceeded to rest camp.	
"	2/5/15	9am	Left rest camp for Pont de Briques Railway Station.	
Pont le Brique	2/5/15	11:30am	Entrained for Merville in same train as Transport and Hqrs. Details which had travelled from Havre.	31 officers 987 others
Merville	2/5/15	3:45pm	Battalion arrived at Merville, detrained and proceeded by march route to Brigade Area, taking up Battn. Headquarters at Bequart Farm at 7 pm. Battalion quartered in farmhouses in the vicinity. Latrine, economy and sanitary arrangements arranged. Divisional Headquarters Guard 1 officer. 30 others mounted at Divisional Headquarters	
Bequart Farm (Robecq)	3/5/15			
WATTEL FARM (Robecq)	4/5/15		Battalion bivouaced in three fields behind this farm for the night.	
LA PIERRE FARM (Robecq)	4/5/15		Billets taken up in neighbouring farms. Signal Office opened for inter-communication.	
"	5/5/15		Battalion at rest. General company training.	
"	6/5/15		" "	
"	7/5/15		" "	
"	8/5/15		Instructions received for battalion to hold itself ready to move at short notice as part of the	

16th A.Y. S. Highrs

WAR DIARY
or
~~INTELLIGENCE SUMMARY~~

Army Form C. 2118.

Place	Date	Hour	Summary of Events and Information	Remarks and references to Appendices
LA PIERRE FARM			General Reserve	
ROBECQ	9/5/15		Battalion still held in general reserve. Route marching and company training carried out. Divine Service	
"	10/5/15		" " " " " " "	
"	11/5/15		Instructions as to time in connection with preparedness to move now withdrawn.	
"	12/5/15		Route marching and company training.	
"	13/5/15		Instructions received to prepare for a move. Divisional Headquarters have dismounted	
"	14/5/15	9 a.m.	Battalion, leading in Brigade, left billets at Robecq for Morris, proceeding thither together with rest of Brigade. Arrived at billets near STRAZEELE at 3 p.m.	30 officers 971 other ranks
STRAZEELE	15/5/15		Battalion at rest in billets. Company training under company arrangements.	
"	16/5/15		Divine Service.	
"	17/5/15		Battalion route march and lectures by company commanders	
"	18/5/15	7 p.m.	Battalion left billets in STRAZEELE and proceeded by march route to VIELLE CHAPELLE arriving there at 4 a.m. Billeted in LA VETU FARM and neighbourhood	
VIELLE CHAPELLE	19/5/15		Companies at disposal of Company Commanders for Drill, Lectures etc. Traffic bend under A.P.M.	2 officers 140 other ranks
"	20/5/15	6.30 p.m.	Battalion left billets and proceeded to DESSAUX MICHEZ FARM, about 3 miles south of VIELLE CHAPELLE. 29 men transferred to 176th (Tunnelling) Coy. R.E.	

WAR DIARY
or
INTELLIGENCE SUMMARY

Army Form C. 2118.

4oth Bn. A. & S. Highrs.

Place	Date	Hour	Summary of Events and Information	Remarks and references to Appendices
LA COUTURE.	21/5/15	6 p.m.	Battalion changed billets. Headquarters at DISSAUX MICHEZ FARM at 8.30 p.m.	
"	22/5/15	9 p.m.	Working party, strength 2 coys, digging communication trenches till 1 a.m. between Reserve and Support Trenches. Trafford Bund shelled in billets by shrapnel.	
"	23/5/15	10 a.m.	First Casualties. 3 men killed, 5 wounded. Working party as before. 1 horse killed by shrapnel.	
"	24/5/15		Working party at night as before.	
"	25/5/15	9 p.m.	B battalion relieved 5th Seaforth in the trenches. Dispositions as follows: A Coy. in Firing Line. B & D. Supports. C in Reserve.	
"	26/5/15		In trenches. Occasional bombardments. Improvement of parapet and parados etc. by sandbags.	
"	27/5/15		Dispositions changed. "C Coy 1 platoon B Coy. in Firing Line. D & 3 platoon A Coy. in support. B. Coy in reserve.	
"	28/5/15		Patrols sent out to reconnoitre German trenches but nothing of importance was seen. Battalion relieved by 5th A. & S. H. about 9 p.m. Proceeded to billets near LOCON for rest.	
LOCON.	29/5/15		Battalion in billets near LOCON in no. 1 Billeting area.	
"	30/5/15	10.30 p.m.	Headquarters and # C & D. Coys. changed billets to make room for 5th A.V.S. Highrs Divine Service.	
"	31/5/15		B. Cleaning up of billets. Regimental Drill. Company training. Total Casualties for Month; 1 officer slightly wounded. 1 officer invalided home. 1 officer slightly wounded, now returned to duty. 4 other ranks killed, 31 wounded, 2 missing.	30 Officers 901 other ranks

Gwlthural LIEUT.-COL.
CMDG. 6TH A&S.S. & SUTH^ND HIGH^RS

2.N.

L. Abraham

121/5931.

51st /5 Division

1/6th A.S.H.
Vol III 1 — 30.6.15.

Conf No 134
152nd Inf Bde

CONFIDENTIAL

War Diary of

1/6th. Battn. Arg. and Suth. Highrs.

from 1st. June, 1915.   to 30th. June, 1915.

(Volume IV)

Army Form C. 2118.
Page 1.

WAR DIARY or INTELLIGENCE SUMMARY

1/6th A. & S. Highrs

Instructions regarding War Diaries and Intelligence Summaries are contained in F. S. Regs., Part II and the Staff Manual respectively. Title pages will be prepared in manuscript.

(Erase heading not required.)

Place	Date	Hour	Summary of Events and Information	Remarks and references to Appendices
LOCON	1/6/15		Battalion in General Reserve of Brigade. Company training. Capt N°Coy l. Col. Watson invalided home.	
"	2/6/15		" " " " " Working party 300 men under Major Hepburn, digging trenches during the night. Visit of Prime Minister to Highland Division. Lieut. J. Macrobert acting adjutant	
"	3/6/15		Headquarters shifted to another farm a few yards away to allow of more room for D Company	
"	4/6/15		Battalion still in General Reserve.	
"	5/6/15		" " " " "	
FESTUBERT (LA QUINQUE RUE)	6/6/15	6 p.m.	Battalion left billets and proceeded to reserve trenches at FESTUBERT (see Sketch) arriving at 9 p.m. approx. Lines G.7.D occupied by battalion while in reserve.	App. I.
"	7/6/15		Occupation of reserve trenches. Repair of earthworks and general improvement of trenches.	
"	8/6/15		Improvement of trenches during daytime. Working party from B.Coy shelled by enemy suffered heavy casualties. Line M.6. M.8. M.9. (French Map. FESTUBERT. 1/10,000). Caps distributed as per attached sketch. Relief completed 2 a.m. approx. 8th Argylls occupied reserve trenches.	1 killed, 1 died of wounds, 10 wounded. App. I.
"	9/6/15	9 p.m.	Relieved 6th Seaforths in fire trenches at D.6.9. ia "Orchard Post." Nearly shelled.	
"	10/6/15		Fire trenches occupied. Improvement of trenches. Heavy thunderstorm during the night of 9/10th. causing breakdown of telephone communication about 3 a.m. Breaks repaired and communication restored by 7.30 a.m. Settled down	
"		9.30 p.m.	Battalion relieved by the Seaforth 6th. Argylls in fire trenches. Relief completed by 3 a.m. Settled down	

Army Form C. 2118.

46th. O.V.S. Hughes

Page 2.

WAR DIARY
or
~~INTELLIGENCE SUMMARY.~~
(Erase heading not required.)

Instructions regarding War Diaries and Intelligence Summaries are contained in F. S. Regs., Part II. and the Staff Manual respectively. Title pages will be prepared in manuscript.

Place	Date	Hour	Summary of Events and Information	Remarks and references to Appendices
LA COUTURE.	10/6/15	5 am.	in billets by 5 am. Battn. now in Brigade Genl. Reserve. Casualties for period of occupation of trenches. 1 Killed, 1 died of wounds. 31 wounded. 27 sent to hospital for various reasons. Several wounded and sick since rejoined.	
"	11/6/15		Battalion in general reserve. Rest and cleaning of person and clothing.	
"	12/6/15		" " " " " " Inspection and ascertaining of deficiencies. 2nd. Lieut'n. Bernet Thomas appointed Adjutant. 2/BN S. STAFFORD REGT. ALBERT	
"	13/6/15		Divine Service. Cleaning up of kit etc.	
"	14/6/15		Battalion in general reserve. Bde. Operation Order No.3 received ordering Battn. to trenches. Bombers in A Line Trench at M.C. (See Sketch Map. App.1) Remainder of Battn. in C.T.D. Line.	
TRENCHES (LA QUINQUE RUE)	14/6/15.		Communication trench completed. 3 trench howitzers and requisite ammunition carried to front trench by party 2nd. Lt. A.T. Thomas joined for duty as Adjutant.	
"	15/6/15	10.30 pm	A. Coy. moved forward to support trench to support 5'th. & 6'th. Seaforths.	
		6.45 pm	80 N.C.O's and men attacked German trenches so event to bombers in conjunction with 5'th & 6'th. Seaforths.	
		11 pm.	Communication trench and wheat parapet repaired by 2 Officers 50 men. Dressing station at Trevery completed by 1 officer 15 men. Battalion in reserve stood to arms during	

Army Form C. 2118.

Page 3

1/6th Bn. Q.V.R.

WAR DIARY
or
INTELLIGENCE SUMMARY.
(Erase heading not required.)

Instructions regarding War Diaries and Intelligence Summaries are contained in F.S. Regs., Part II. and the Staff Manual respectively. Title pages will be prepared in manuscript.

Place	Date	Hour	Summary of Events and Information	Remarks and references to Appendices
TRENCHES (LA QUINQUE ROE)	16/6/15		remainder of the night.	
		11p.	A. Coy in support trenches. B. Coy in reserve trenches. Sanitary arrangements in reserve trenches improved. Trenches and dug-outs improved. Parapets repaired in fire trench by 2 officers 80 men	
"	17/6/15	7.30am	Operation order 13 No. 210 ordering relief. Indian Communication Trench not to be used.	
		9.45pm	5th A. 1. H. arrives at Indian Village and relieves B. C. & D. Coys in 6" D. Line. (App. 1) Conference	
		11.15pm	ordered to meet in relief of 5 Ch. 7 6th. Seaforths in Fire Trenches. Dispositions as shewn on	
"	18/6/15	7am.	Appendix 1. Relief in position by 12 midnight. Carrier pigeon reported sent up from German trenches towards	
			our trenches. Afterm. position of enemy heavy howitzer battery reported and passed to Bde. Hqrs. Orchard	
		4.30am	trenches shelled for 30 minutes, portion of parapet being blown in. This was at once repaired. Working party	
			from A. Coy. assisting engineers throughout the night. Learch party discovered 6 dead in front of M.G. and (App.1)	
			buried them there during the night. German M.G. fired at our trenches M.6 about 27B8.3 at 6.20pm.	
	19/6/15	7.30am 8am	60 yds. parapet in orchard damaged in morning by shell fire. Our own shells burst 100 yds behind fire trench. Support trench shelled with high explosive, parapet blown in but afterwards repaired. All now worked hard throughout the day and partly through the night	

Army Form C. 2118.
Page 4.

WAR DIARY
or
INTELLIGENCE SUMMARY.
(Erase heading not required.)

/6th. Bn. A.Y.S.H

Instructions regarding War Diaries and Intelligence Summaries are contained in F.S. Regs., Part II. and the Staff Manual respectively. Title pages will be prepared in manuscript.

Place	Date	Hour	Summary of Events and Information	Remarks and references to Appendices
TRENCHES (LA QUINQUE RUE)	19/4/15	3h.	A. Coy. moved into Indian Communication Trench and D. Coy. closer to allow our guns to bombard M 10 from 3pm to 6pm. Vacant trenches re-occupied immediately after bombardment. Enemy reported moving M 28, K 12, L 23, J 28. (Trench map FESTUBERT 1/10000). Enemy M.G. mounted 2500 yds. W. of M 15. German trenches and wire at orchard not damaged by our shell fire. Enemy	
		4pm	trench mortar silenced by our shell fire. Parapets at M 9, M 8, M 6, damaged by hostile shell fire. C.R.E. infantry work done by our men and appeared satisfactory with out done.	
"	20/4/15	9am } 10-30am}	Bombardment of M10 continued. A + D. Coys. moving as before. Support trench shelled most of the day by high explosive shrapnel.	
		9pm	Battalion relieved in front trenches by 6th (A.P.) Highrs, all companies clear of front trench by 12 midnight. Companies proceeded independently to billets in second line trenches near LE TOURET.	
LE TOURET			at X 17 a. (BETHUNE). Casualties for period in trenches:- Killed, 16, Wounded, 62.	
"	21/4/15		Battalion at rest. Cleaning up of clothing and equipment. Deficiencies being completed.	
"	22/4/15		Inspection of ammunition, iron rations, equipment etc and completion of deficiencies. Battalion moved to new billeting area at Q. 22 d 4.3. at 5 pm.	
QUENTIN.				

1577 Wt.W10791/1773 500,000 1/15 D.D.&L. A.D.S.S./Forms/C. 2118.

Army Form C. 2118.
Page 5

1/6th A.V.S. Highrs.

WAR DIARY
or
~~INTELLIGENCE SUMMARY.~~
(Erase heading not required.)

Instructions regarding War Diaries and Intelligence Summaries are contained in F.S. Regs., Part II. and the Staff Manual respectively. Title pages will be prepared in manuscript.

Place	Date	Hour	Summary of Events and Information	Remarks and references to Appendices
QUENTIN	23/6/15		Battalion at rest. Deficiencies in ammunition, respirators and iron rations completed under Company Commanders. All available officers present at lecture and demonstration on use of chlorine gas by chief gas expert.	
"	24/6/15		Company training under company commanders. 15 officers visited and attended lecture on Engineering Trench Works. Battalion moved to Second Line Reserve Trenches at LE TOURET. Large working parties at trenches during the night.	
LE TOURET	24/6/15			
QUENTIN	25/6/15	10.30am	Battalion moved back to old billets at Q.22.d.4.3 arriving 1.30 pm. Order received to join remainder of Brigade at ESTAIRES on 26th inst.	
ESTAIRES	26/6/15	9am	Battalion proceeded to billets in ESTAIRES arriving 1pm. Companies billeted in various parts of the town. Regimental staff officers visited portion of reserve trenches to be taken over by battalion, at M.6.d.2.0. (Sheet 36)	
"	27/6/15	11am	Divine Service. 7pm. Battalion left to take over Reserve Trenches at M.6.d.2.0.(Reference Sheet 36) from 2nd. Scottish Rifles. Trenches and Posts taken over by 10 pm. Posts 17, 18 and 19 already taken over at 3 pm.	

Army Form C. 2118.

Page 6.

WAR DIARY
or
INTELLIGENCE SUMMARY.

(Erase heading not required.)

4th A. & S. Highrs.

Instructions regarding War Diaries and Intelligence Summaries are contained in F.S. Regs., Part II. and the Staff Manual respectively. Title pages will be prepared in manuscript.

Place	Date	Hour	Summary of Events and Information	Remarks and references to Appendices
M.G.D.2.0	28/6/15		No. 91, Pte. W. Proctor and No. 3999, Pte. E. Palmer recommended for D.C.M. for deeds of gallantry at FESTUBERT on 15th inst. 3162, Pte. W. Carlile (killed) recommended for V.C. on 15th inst. Machine Gun Detachment received special mention for gallantry and devotion to duty. 2nd. Lieut. S.L. Hardie and Sgt. A. Stewart (wounded) being specially recommended. Fatigue parties supplied for carrying R.E. stores to fire trench from M6 D.i.3. Battalion held in Brigade Reserve.	APP. II.
"	29/6/15			
"	30/6/15		Battalion held in Brigade Reserve. Working parties for carrying tools, sand-bags and ratins to Fire Trench. Improvement of sanitation in Reserve Billets. Casualties for month, killed, 18. Wounded 93. Sick sent to Field Ambulance 104. Returned to Duty 74. Strength, 30th. June, 1915. 30 officers, 740 other ranks.	

R. Stewart Myer
for LIEUT.-COL.
CMDG. 6TH ARG. & SUTHND HIGHRS

APPENDIX II

COPY.

CORPS. REGISTER NO.

152nd Infantry Brigade 51st (Highland) Division H.Q. Corps

SCHEDULE NO. TO BE LEFT BLANK	UNIT	REGT. NO.	NAME AND RANK	ACTION FOR WHICH RECOMMENDED	RECOMMENDED BY	REWARD OR HONOUR	TO BE LEFT BLANK
	1/6th Argyll & Sutherland Highlanders	91	Pte. Proctor, William	Dressing a wounded man under heavy shell fire and then carrying the man on his back to cover of trenches under heavy shell fire thereby saving the man's life	L/T McPherson O/C 1/6 A.& S. Highrs	Distinguished Conduct Medal	
	1/6th Argyll & Sutherland Highlanders.	3999	Pte. Palmer, G.	Dressing two wounded men under heavy shell fire and then getting them under cover thereby probably saving the men's lives	L/T McPherson O/C 1/6 A.& S. Highrs	Distinguished Conduct Medal.	
	1/6th Argyll & Sutherland Highlanders	3162	Pte. Carlyle, W. (Killed in Action, 15th June, 1915)	When the advance on the German trenches was arrested (the bombing escort being then about 100 yards from the German lines) proceeded from the fire trench into the open under heavy machine gun and rifle fire and held fire and burst of enemy's wounds (Ppl. J. Kelley) being killed whilst doing so.	L/T McPherson O/C 1/6 A.& S. Highrs	Victoria Cross	

APPENDIX II.

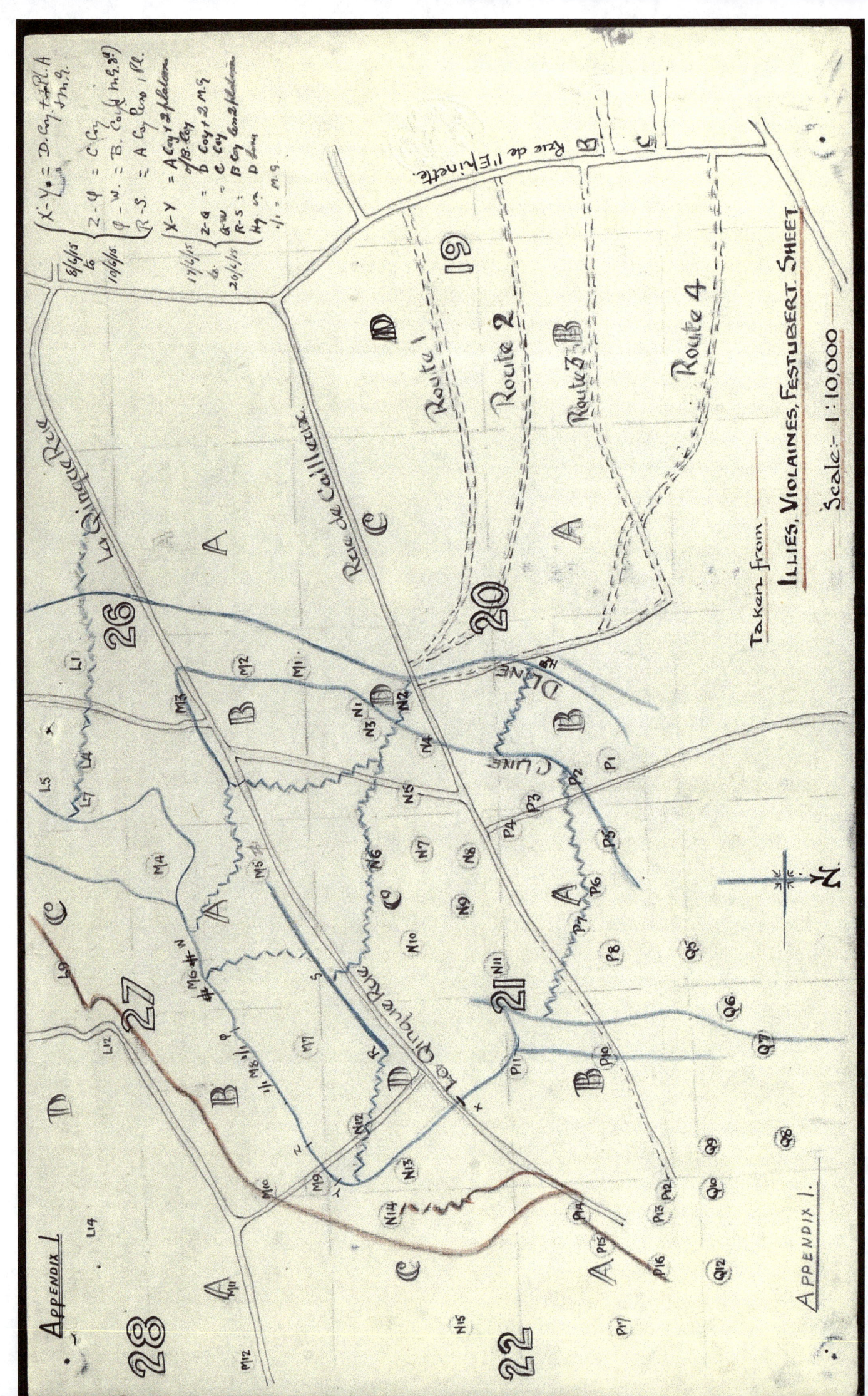

APPENDIX 1.

J.77.

Headquarters
152nd Infantry Brigade

Recommendation vide your 561 dated 24th June 1915 is forwarded herewith.

The attached report from 2nd Lieut. Stephen Lindsay Hardie is forwarded for your information and recommendation for rewards as you consider necessary.

There is no doubt that the Machine Gun Section Commanded by 2nd Lieutenant Stephen Lindsay Hardie acted in a most gallant manner during the evening of 15th June 1915 during the action near Festubert when they covered the advance of the 154th Brigade and 1/5th Battalion Seaforth Highlanders.

It is known that heavy casualties were caused in the enemy's ranks by the gallant action of this detachment.

It will be noted that one gun was stripped in the open

and again brought into Action,
and fired until the action
was over. N.C.O.'s and men
of the Machine Gun detachment
were severely wounded, 1334
Sergt A Stewart (Machine Gun Sergeant)
losing his eyesight.
The Machine Gun detachment under
2nd Lieut Hardie worked continuously
on making a new Machine Gun
Emplacement from daybreak on the
15th June 1915 until the Action
commenced which certainly saved
the guns from being destroyed
by the enemy's shell fire.
I would particularly bring to your notice
2nd Lieut Hardie and Sergt A Stewart
who Commanded the Machine Gun detachment
15th   5

28/6/15.   Jas. S. Stewart

S.N.

51st Division

121/6358

11th A&S.H
1/0
1-31-7-15

Volume V

Confidential.

War Diary
of
1/6th A.V. & S. Highrs

From 1st July 1915 To 31st July 1915.

Vol.V

Army Form C. 2118.
Page 1.

1/6th A.V.S. Highrs.

WAR DIARY
or
~~INTELLIGENCE SUMMARY.~~

Place	Date	Hour	Summary of Events and Information	Remarks and references to Appendices
(Sheet 36) M.C.D.2.0	1/7/15		Battalion held in Brigade Reserve in reserve billets.	
		5.30pm	Draft of 80 N.C.Os and men arrived at Battn. Hqrs from ROUEN and posted to Companies in following proportions. A. Coy. 41, B. Coy. 14, C. Coy. 14, D. 11.	30 officers 740 others
"	2/7/15		Battalion held in Brigade Reserve in reserve billets.	30 officers 828 others
		9 am	Draft inspected G.O.C. 152nd Inf. Bde. at Br. Hqrs.	
"	3/7/15	4.30 a	Stretcher bearers summoned to assist 5th. A.V.S.H.	
		9.15 pm	Battalion paraded by companies which proceeded independently to Fire Trenches at F Lines (See Sketch) relieving 5th A.V.S.H. All companies reported in position by 11.15 pm. Serious shortage of ammunition reported in Fire Trench. This was afterwards made up by drawing from S.A.A. Depot. Lieut. Col. J.S. Stewart placed on sick list.	Appx. 1
"	4/7/15		Position shelled for an hour during the day. Little activity in enemy lines. Lieut. J. Mac Robert placed in charge of snipers. Sniping posts arranged by him. General improvement of trenches. Dug outs constructed at Battn. Hqrs. Patrols and listening posts out during the night. German patrol approached our barbed wire.	

16th Bn. A. & S. Highrs.

WAR DIARY
or
INTELLIGENCE SUMMARY

Army Form C. 2118.
Page 2

Place	Date	Hour	Summary of Events and Information	Remarks and references to Appendices
M.G.D.2.0	4/7/15		German aeroplanes reconnoitred our position. Carrier pigeons liberated by enemy.	
"	5/7/15		German sniper hit at Point 370. by one of our men. Damage done to parapet at A Coy's portion of line. by H.E. Grass cutting in front of parapet commenced. M.G. emplacement completed. Draft occupied in making dug outs at M.6.D.2.0. also instructed in musketry.	
"	6/7/15	11 pm	Enemy rifle fire opened on our working parties but silenced by rapid fire, rifle grenade no.3. Over 200 H.E. shells fell on A Coy's portion of the line doing considerable damage to parapet and parados. Very heavy rain during the night. Reported sent at on this account. 40 yds of grass cut in front of fire trenches. Instructions issued in case of attack as to rendezvous of all employed men. Captain R.A.M.C. Haldane very wisely closed his company in to B-By. during heavy hill fire. leaving only an observation post in his Fire Trench. thus saving many men from being killed or wounded. Bombardment lasted from 7 am till 4:30 pm	

WAR DIARY
~~INTELLIGENCE SUMMARY~~

Army Form C. 2118.
Page 3

1/6th A.V.S. Highrs

Place	Date	Hour	Summary of Events and Information	Remarks and references to Appendices
M 6 D. 2.0	8/7/15	12.25am	Considerable rifle fire from Lesforks on right. This was replied to by enemy who we fire opened to our Trenches. A. Coy. replied but firing died down about 1.10am. Damaged communication trench at F3 fully repaired. 200 yds of grass cut in front of Fire Trench. Actual number of rifles in Fire Trench, 508. Major H.C. Donald R.A.M.C. and Lieut. D.S. Allan. placed on the sick list.	
"	8/7/15		Situation quiet during the day. Building and repair of parapet continued. Machine Gun emplacements constructed. Arrangements made for relief of battalion.	
"	9/7/15	9pm	Relief commenced. Battalion relieved in Fire Trenches by 1/8th Liverpool Regt. Relief completed by 10.30 pm. Battalion proceeded to rest billets at LA GORGUE arriving 1am on 9th. Casualties for period in Trenches. 1 killed. 17 wounded 15 to sent hospital. Battalion at rest as part of Brigade in reserve to Division. Cleaning of person and clothing. A.V.B. Coy. visited Divisional Baths for cleaning purposes.	
LA GORGUE.	10/7/15			
"	11/7/15	10am	Divine Service. Cleaning of clothing and equipment continued. Two working parties each 1 officer and 100 men supplied for work with Anglesey Siege Coy. R.E. at M 6 D. 3.3.	

Army Form C. 2118.
Page 4.

WAR DIARY
or
INTELLIGENCE SUMMARY.
(Erase heading not required.)

16th Bn. A. & S. Highrs

Instructions regarding War Diaries and Intelligence Summaries are contained in F.S. Regs., Part II. and the Staff Manual respectively. Title pages will be prepared in manuscript.

Place	Date	Hour	Summary of Events and Information	Remarks and references to Appendices
LA GORGUE	12/7/15		Captain J.A.C. Swan placed on sick list to-day.	
"	13/7/15	7pm	Battalion at rest. 7pm. Battalion Headquarters and A. Coy. moved to G.32.a.2.2. Working party of 150 men supplied for work with 1/1st Highland Field Coy. R.E.	
"			Battalion at rest. Lt. & Qr. Mr. J.A. Thomson, placed on sick list to-day. Lieut. J.A.S. Shanks assumed duties of Quartermaster to-day. Lieut. W. Phillips, R.A.M.C. joined for duty as Medical Officer vice Major A.E.D. Malot affairs selected for duty at HAVRE. Copies of Alarm Orders issued to Coy. M.S. Transport, Bombers.	
"	14/7/15		Lieut. L.L. Hardie took over duties of Bat. M.S. Officer in place of Cpt. S. McLardie, on sick list.	
"	"	7pm	Working party, 150 strong, supplied for work under R.E. Operation Order No. 7. received ordering reliefs to take place	
LAVENTIE.	15/7/15	9.30am	Working party, 150 strong, supplied for work under R.E. Battalion in reserve.	
"	16/7/15		Working party 50 strong, supplied for work under R.E. Coy. in Post 10. shelled heavily at intervals during the night. Battalion in reserve. Lieut. Col. J.S. STEWART, having returned from Hospital resumed command of the Battalion.	
"	17/7/15		2 men killed and 5 men wounded at 152nd Infantry Brigade Bomb School Cy.	

Army Form C. 2118.
Page 5.

WAR DIARY
or
~~INTELLIGENCE SUMMARY~~

(Erase heading not required.)

46th Bn. A.I.F. Nights

Instructions regarding War Diaries and Intelligence Summaries are contained in F. S. Regs., Part II. and the Staff Manual respectively. Title pages will be prepared in manuscript.

Place	Date	Hour	Summary of Events and Information	Remarks and references to Appendices
LAVENTIE	18/4/15		accidental explosion of a hand grenade while being instructed in the use of grenades. Captain A. Craig attached to 2/2nd. Field Coy. R.E. for rations and billets while employed on construction of 2nd.Y. 4th. Line Defences. 2/Lieut. D.S.ALLAN & Capt. J.McLARDIE sent to Base Hospital, Boulogne. Working party 50 strong supplied for work under R.E. Battalion in Reserve. Work on dug outs and parapets at Posts 10, 11, & 12.	Appx II
"	19/4/15		Battalion in Reserve. Work on dug outs and parapets at Posts 10, 11, & 12. Captain J.H.C. SWAN returned to duty from Hospital. Working party 50 strong supplied for work under R.E. 1368 Pte. F. Wilson awarded 56 days. Field Imprisonment No.1. for sleeping on his post. 4206 Pte. R. Grant " " " " " " " " 3145 Pte. McKay sentenced to 1 years Imprisonment with hard labour for assaulting a N.C.O. in discharge of his duty, Brig. Gen. Comdg. 152nd. Inf. Bde. recommends that the sentence be suspended.	
"	20/4/15		Battalion in Reserve. Work on dug outs and parapets at Posts 10, 11, & 12. Working party 50 strong supplied for work under R.E.	

WAR DIARY

or INTELLIGENCE SUMMARY

Army Form C. 2118.
Page 6.

16th Bn. A. & S. Highrs.

Place	Date	Hour	Summary of Events and Information	Remarks and references to Appendices
LAVENTIE	21/7/15		Battalion in Reserve. Operation Order No.8 issued. Improvement of dug outs and parapets. Working party 4 officers 100 men supplied for work under R.E.	
"	22/7/15		Battalion in Reserve. Operation Order No.8 received 8am ordering reliefs. Battn. Hqrs. A. & Y. & Coys. left Reserve Billets at LAVENTIE at 10 p.m. and proceeded to Billets at K.12.A.1.1. (Sheet 36a) near VIERHOUCK. D. Coy. relieved by 3rd. London Regt. proceeded to billets independently. March to billets under heavy rain.	
VIERHOUCK	23/7/15		Battalion at rest. Cleaning arms and equipment after heavy rain. No. 1619 Pte. Allan Gilmour sentenced to 9 months H.L. (3 months commuted) for sleeping on his post.	
"	24/7/15		Battalion at rest. Companies at disposal of Coy. Commanders	
"	25/7/15		Battalion at rest. Arrangements made for entrainment of Battalion.	
"	26/7/15	1p.	Battalion marched to LA GORGUE where it entrained for CORBIE at 4 p.m. Route travelled was via	

Army Form C. 2118.

WAR DIARY
or
INTELLIGENCE SUMMARY.
(Erase heading not required.)

Instructions regarding War Diaries and Intelligence Summaries are contained in F. S. Regs., Part II. and the Staff Manual respectively. Title pages will be prepared in manuscript.

Place	Date	Hour	Summary of Events and Information	Remarks and references to Appendices
LA HOUSSOYE	28/7/15		MERVILLE - HAZEBROUCK - ST. OMER - CALAIS (Arrived 8pm; halt for refreshments; journey resumed 9pm.) BOULOGNE - ABBEVILLE (Halt for refreshments) AMIENS - CORBIE. Arrived at CORBIE 5am. Proceeded by march route to LA HOUSSOYE 6am arriving at Billets 8am. In area of concentration. Inspection of battalion by G.O.C. III Army. Draft 20 strong arrived from Base Depot, ETAPLES. Personnel (except 2 men) consisted of men rejoining battalion from Hospital. Major W. McK. HEPBURN, placed on sick list.	
"	29/7/15	5:30pm	Battalion proceeded by march route to forward billets at MARTINSART arriving 11:30pm. Company Commanders and M.S. Officer visited French trenches about to be taken over by battalion.	
"	30/7/15	12 midnight	Battalion marched to trenches at AUTHUILLE to take over trenches from 116th French Regt. Relief completed and battalion in position by 4:30am.	
AUTHUILLE	31/7/15		Battalion in fire trenches. Companies arranged as follows. B.C.D. in Fire Trenches. A. Coy in support. 65,000 rounds of ammunition carried up to Fire Trenches. Enemy Trenches from 50 to 200 yds. apart.	

R. Stewart (?) LIEUT.-COL.
CMDG. 6TH ARG. & SUTH. HIGHRS

Army Form C. 2118.

WAR DIARY
or
~~INTELLIGENCE SUMMARY.~~
(Erase heading not required.)

116th A.& S.H.

Instructions regarding War Diaries and Intelligence Summaries are contained in F. S. Regs., Part II. and the Staff Manual respectively. Title pages will be prepared in manuscript.

Place	Date	Hour	Summary of Events and Information	Remarks and references to Appendices
AUTHOUILLE	31/7/15		The Officer Commanding 116th French Infantry Regt. complimented the battalion on the excellent manner in which the relief of the French Battalion was carried out on the night of 30/31st July. The French commander recognition and two subalterns remained in trenches with Battalion for two days. The French commander (———) held a meeting of officers of the Battalion and impressed on them the importance of a good system of sanitation being kept up in the trenches and for the necessity of all ranks by day and night being the utmost vigilance. The French trenches, defences and sanitary arrangements are the best yet taken over by the Battalion in France, entailing many months of hard work and thought, Full throught.	

R. Stewart ___ LIEUT.-COL.
CMDG. 6TH ARG. & SUTH'D HIGH'RS

1577 Wt. W10791/1773 500,000 1/15 D. D. & L. A.D.S.S./Forms/C. 2118.

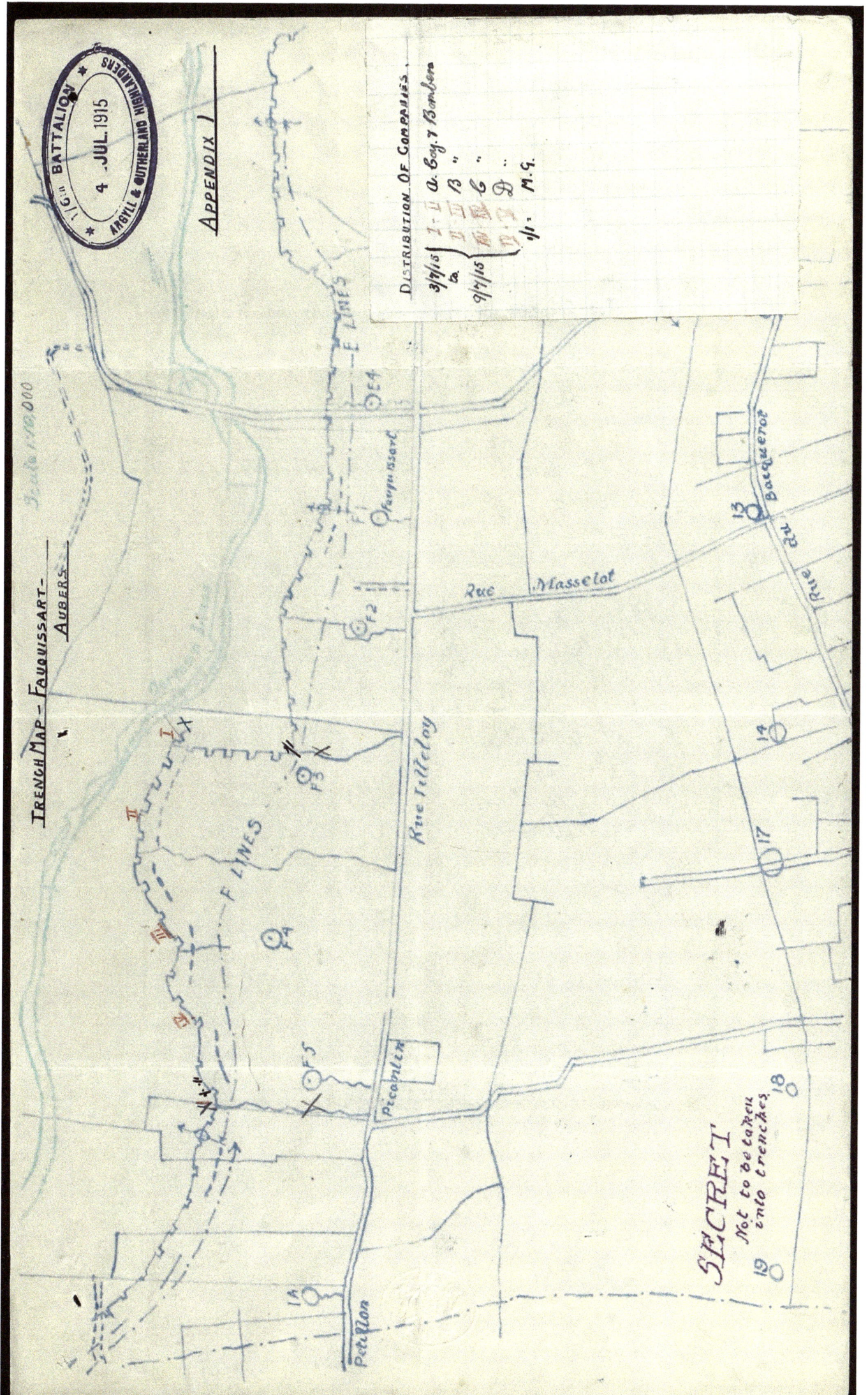

To Adjt 1/6 A & S Hrs

I beg to report the following casualties which were due to the accidental explosion of a grenade.

Killed

1809	L/Cpl Love J	B Coy
1617	Pte Connely G.	C Coy

Wounded

18	Sgt McCallum D		C Coy
2023	Pte Kerr W		C Coy
2570	Pte Williamson J		C Coy
3075	Pte Mutrie R		C Coy
3367	L/Cpl Marshall W		C Coy

APPENDIX II.

R.A. Milne
Lieut
O.C. Batt. Grenadiers

CONFIDENTIAL
No. 134
152 INF. BDE.

CONFIDENTIAL.
-o-o-o-o-o-o-

W A R   D I A R Y

of

1/6th. Battn. Arg. and Suth'd. Highrs.

From, 1st. Aug.1915 To, 31st. Aug. 1915.

16th Bn. O.& S. Highrs.   Vol. VI
                                                           Army Form C. 2118.
                                                           Page 1

WAR DIARY
or
INTELLIGENCE SUMMARY.
(Erase heading not required.)

Instructions regarding War Diaries and Intelligence Summaries are contained in F. S. Regs., Part II. and the Staff Manual respectively. Title pages will be prepared in manuscript.

Place	Date	Hour	Summary of Events and Information	Remarks and references to Appendices
AUTHUILLE 1/8/15	1/8/15		Battalion in Fire Trenches. All defences manned and protective measures taken in expectation of German attack. Battalion stood to arms during the night.	
"	2/8/15		Battalion in Fire Trenches. Protective measures in case of attack. Lieuts. J.H. Brown and 2/Lieuts. J.H.E. Coats and W. Forsyth who arrived in let inst. are posted to companies as follows. Lieut. J.H. Brown to C. Coy. 2/Lieut. J.H.E. Coats to D Coy. and 2/Lieut. W. Forsyth to B. Coy. Capt. J.H.C. Swan placed on Sick List.	
"	3/8/15		Battalion in Fire Trenches. No activity manifested on part of the enemy. The three companies in Fire Trenches each send out nightly a small patrol under an Officer or N.C.O. to watch for signs of activity on the part of the enemy. These patrols even though they bring in no information. have been found to stimulate the offensive spirit among the men and thus serve a useful purpose.	
"	4/8/15		Battalion in Fire Trenches. Situation all quiet. Patrols out at night exploring the front. Capt. R.H.B. Haldane on leave from 4/8/15 — 12/8/15.	

Army Form C. 2118.

Page 2

1/6th. Bn. A.Y.S. Highrs

WAR DIARY
or
INTELLIGENCE SUMMARY.
(Erase heading not required.)

Instructions regarding War Diaries and Intelligence Summaries are contained in F. S. Regs., Part II. and the Staff Manual respectively. Title pages will be prepared in manuscript.

Place	Date	Hour	Summary of Events and Information	Remarks and references to Appendices
AUTHUILE	5/8/15		Battalion in Fire Trenches. Situation quiet on both our own and enemy's front.	
"	6/8/15		Battalion in Fire Trenches. Sniping of enemy continued. Patrols out at night.	
"	7/8/15		Battalion in Fire Trenches. Disposition of Companies shown on Sketch Map attached. Machine Guns on right of sector.	Appx. 1.
"	8/8/15		Battalion in Fire Trenches. Situation quiet all over. Patrols out examining wire and listening for signs of enemy.	
"	9/8/15		Battalion in Fire Trenches. During the night a very heavy Thunderstorm occurred doing some damage to Fire Trenches by washing away earth etc.	
"	10/8/15		Battalion in Fire Trenches. Situation quiet.	
"	11/8/15		Battalion in Fire Trenches. About 7pm and again at 10-30 pm, enemy fired mortar bombs	

1577 Wt.W10791/1773 500,000 1/15 D.D. & L. A.D.S.S./Forms/C. 2118.

WAR DIARY
or
INTELLIGENCE SUMMARY.

Army Form C. 2118.

Page 3

950/16th A.Y. & Highrs.

Place	Date	Hour	Summary of Events and Information	Remarks and references to Appendices
AUTHUILLE	12/8/15		Captain A. CRAIG and 2/Lieut. J.D. HURST placed on the Sick List. Battalion in Fire Trenches. Officers of 18th. Lancers and Deccan Horse conducted over Fire Trenches previous to relief.	
"	13/8/15		Battalion in Fire Trenches. Preparation for relief of Battn. by 18th. Lancers and Deccan Horse.	
		9.30pm	Relief commenced.	
		12.30pm 14/8/15	Relief finished. Battalion proceeded independently by companies to billets in BRESLE arriving about 4am, 14.i.t.	
BRESLE.	14/8/15		Battalion at rest. Casualties for period in Trenches. 2 killed, 2 died of wounds, 9 wounded.	
"	15/8/15		Battalion at rest. Cleaning of men's persons and clothing after period in trenches	
"	16/8/15		Battalion at rest. Companies at disposal of Company Commanders.	
"	17/8/15		Battalion at rest. Inspection of Companies by C.O. when all companies were found to be clean and well turned out. Captain A. CRAIG reported for duty from Hospital. Lieut. R.S. MILNE placed on sick list	
"	18/8/15		Battalion at rest. Battalion paraded in marching order at 10am to G.O.C. being present on parade. Gas demonstration by gas expert III. Army	

WAR DIARY or INTELLIGENCE SUMMARY

Army Form C. 2118.
Page 4

16th Bn. A.I.S.H.

Place	Date	Hour	Summary of Events and Information	Remarks and references to Appendices
BRESLE	19/8/15		Battalion at rest. Companies at disposal of Company Officers for Musketry Close Order Drill. Bathing Parades etc. Lieut. HARDIE appointed Bde. M.G. Officer.	
"	20/8/15		Battalion at rest. Orders received for Battalion to proceed to Fire Trenches. Company Commanders visited trenches, preparatory to taking over. Detailed report on system of Discipline and Interior Economy in fire trenches sent to Bde. Hqrs.	APP. II.
"	21/8/15	9 a.m.	C.O. visited fire trench, preparatory to taking over.	
		4 p.m.	Battalion paraded in marching order and proceeded to fire trenches via DERNANCOURT — MOULIN DE VIVIER — ALBERT — BÉCOURT — LA BOISSELLE. Battalion relieved 5th. London about 11 p.m., all reliefs completed by 11.30 p.m. Dispositions shown on sketch map attached	APP. III.
LA BOISSELLE	22/8/15		A. Coy and the left of B. Coy are situated in advanced trench within twenty yards of German trenches. Hand grenades are used extensively by both sides; Germans fired several aerial torpedoes which landed harmlessly behind our lines. This is the first time that this Battalion has experienced these weapons & their French circles	

WAR DIARY

1/6th Bn. A.& S.H.

Army Form C. 2118.

Page 5.

Instructions regarding War Diaries and Intelligence Summaries are contained in F. S. Regs., Part II. and the Staff Manual respectively. Title pages will be prepared in manuscript.

(Erase heading not required.)

Place	Date	Hour	Summary of Events and Information	Remarks and references to Appendices
LA BOISSELLE	23/8/15		Battalion in Fire Trenches. Mortar bombardment of A. Coy. trenches. Grenade fighting on left flank. Sniping organized under 2/Lieut. L.L. SHEARER. Machine Guns under Lieut. D.N. DRYBROUGH. Battn. M.G. Officer.	
"	24/8/15		Battalion in Fire Trenches. Mine exploded by our men, damaging German trenches. Captain J. MAC ROBERT wounded in leg and side by rifle grenade while conducting 2/Lieut. J.O. LANG round trench occupied by A. Coy. preparatory to handing over to B. Coy. 2/Lieut. J.O. LANG also wounded in the foot. During period the Battalion is in Fire Trenches, daily Progress Reports, recording all that has happened during previous 24 hours, are submitted each morning by Coy. Commanders. These reports are consolidated and forwarded to Bde. Hqrs. Specimen report attached. 2/Lieut. E. MacKECHNIE joined for duty with Battn.	APP. IV.
"	25/8/15		Battalion in Fire Trenches. Dispositions of Companies rearranged as follows. Right: Coy. A. Coy., Centre Coy. C. Coy., Left Coy. B. Coy. Our Machine Gun Section Right up burst of fire on Transport heard moving at LA BOISSELLE. Little activity on part of the enemy during the night.	

WAR DIARY
or
INTELLIGENCE SUMMARY.

Army Form C. 2118.
Page 6.

#6th Bn. A.I.S. Highrs

Place	Date	Hour	Summary of Events and Information	Remarks and references to Appendices
LA BOISELLE	26/8/15		Battalion in Fire Trenches. Quiet night over whole of sector. Part of parapet of DONOLLOU TRENCH blown in but re-built. 2/Lieuts. R. SHANKS and W.A.S. BROWN joined for duty with Battalion on 26/8/15.	M/Lieut
"	27/8/15		Battalion in Fire Trenches. Very quiet night. A few mortar shells fired by enemy doing little damage. Between 10 p.m. and 12 midnight several rifle grenades fired by enemy at left of our sector. Summarized statement of strength returns rendered during month attached	M/Lieut App. V
"	28/8/15		Battalion in Fire Trenches. Situation quiet. About 8.30 p.m. heavy thunderstorm burst and continued during part of the night. Trenches flooded and work stopped. Enemy evidently nervy owing to darkness, sent up many flares throughout the night.	M/Lieut
"	29/8/15		Battalion in Fire Trenches. Dispositions of Companies re-arranged as follows:- Right: Coy. B Coy. Centre Coy. A Coy. Left Coy. C. Coy. Situation quiet during the night. Heavy rain again flooded communication trenches.	

Army Form C. 2118.

Page 7.

WAR DIARY
or
INTELLIGENCE SUMMARY.

(Erase heading not required.)

1/6th Bn. A.&S. Highrs.

Place	Date	Hour	Summary of Events and Information	Remarks and references to Appendices
LA BOISSELLE	30/8/15		Battalion in Fire Trenches. A number of Mortar Bombs fell on the left of our sector between the hours of 4.30 p.m. and 7.40 p.m. Our artillery retaliated with two H.E. shells from Howitzers and three Shrapnel from Field Guns. Operation Order No. 14. received from Brigade Hqrs. ordering relief. Battalion in Fire Trenches. Draft of 13 men arrived from ETAPLES to rejoin Battalion.	
"	31/8/15	8 pm		

Casualties for August, 1915:-   Killed & Died of Wounds 7. other ranks
             Wounded, 2 officers, 23 other ranks.
             Sick, 67 other ranks
             Died, 1 other rank.

Signed LIEUT.-COL.
CMDG. 6TH ARG. & SUTHD HIGHRS

CONFIDENTIAL.

WAR DIARY-1/6th. A. & S. HIGHRS.

APPENDICES.

APPENDIX 1, Sketch Plan of THIEPVAL Trenches.

APPENDIX, 2, Report on Discipline and Interior Economy of Battalion while in the Trenches.

APPENDIX, 3 Sketch Plan of LA BOISSELLE Trenches.

APPENDIX 4, Specimen Progress Report.

APPENDIX, 5, Summary of Weekly States for Month.

Appendix I.

REFERENCE:- Plan Directeur D.B.S. 1/20000

PARC.

	FIRE TRENCHES
	COMM: TRENCHES, SAPS Etc
---	UNDERGROUND
....	OLD TRENCHES
S	SAPS for LISTENING Etc.
P	OBS. & SNIPING POSTS
Q	SHELL PROOF OBS. POSTS
MG	MACHINE GUN EMPLACEMENTS
A	O.C. 'A' COY
C	" 'C' "
D	" 'D' "
CO	COMMANDING OFFICER (Small Letter Denotes Coy.)
T	TELEPHONES
X	END OF, OR JUNCTION OF COYS
✚	DRESSING STATION
O	ORDERLY ROOM

APPROX. SCALE 1/2000

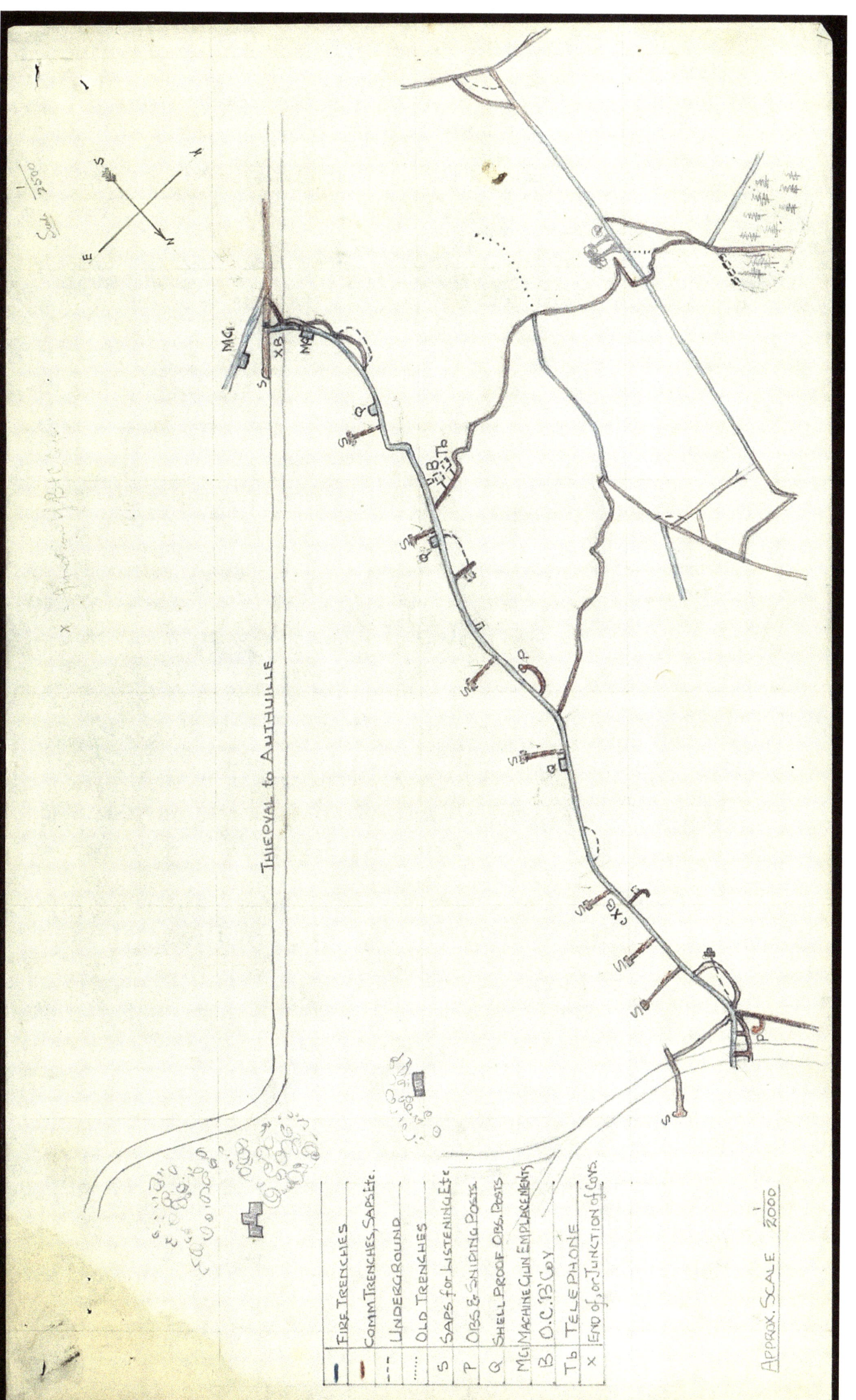

COPY.   Appendix II.

Headquarters,
    152nd. Infantry Brigade.
1 Please forward a report on the system of discipline and interior
economy in force in each of the Battalions under your Command when they are
in the fire trenches, by 9 a.m. on 22nd. August, 1915 for the information
of the General Officer Commanding.

2   The report is to be drawn up under the following headings in the
order given . Other headings may be added on any points coming within
the scope of the report which you may wish to bring to notice.

(a) Posting and relief of sentries.
(b) Arrangements for sleep and rest for men who are to be on sentry duty.
(c) Arrest and confinement of men accused of serious offences.
(d) Disposal of accused by Company Commanders and by Commanding Officers.
(e) Warning of accused for trial.
(f) Assistance and advice to accused brought before Field General Courts
Martial.
(g) Responsibility and power of Platoon Commander.
(h) Prevention of straggling to the rear.
(i) Warning of men for trench duty and steps taken to have evidence to
support a charge of desertion should a man absent himself from trench duty
(j) Discipline and Interior Economy of men remaining with 1st. Line
Transport.
(k) Cooking and distribution of rations.
(l) Supply of drinking water to the trenches.
(m) Precautions against gas. Men detailed to charge of vermoral sprayers.
(n) Inspection of rifles ,ammunition, kits etc.
(o) Arrangements for sending kits of men admitted to Field Ambulances with
or after them.
(p) Detailing of fatigues and working parties.
(q) Publication of orders which concern the men and how made known to the
men.
(r) Supply and issue of fuel. Distribution of braziers.
(s) Inspection of personnel, horses and vehicles of 1st. Line Transport
going on duty.
(t) Care and cleansing of water carts and protection of water supply.
(u) Sanitation in the trenches.
(v) Instruction in cleaning of rifles and prevention of self inflicted
wounds.
(w) Protection of food fromXXXXXXX flies and burial or destruction of
refuse.

                                    (Sgd) A.J.G. Moir, Lt. Col.,
                                                A.A. & Q.M.G.,
18th. August, 1915.   51st. (H) Division.

            COPY OF REPLY SENT TO ABOVE BY

            1/6th. Bn. Arg. and Suth'd. Highrs.

Headquarters,
    152nd. Infantry Brigade.
Herewith report called for in your No. 1076 d/18th. inst.
(a)   Reliefs are told off by Platoon Commanders and Platoon Sergt.
and are posted and relieved by the N.C.O. in charge of Section every hour
or half hour depending on nature of post and proximity of the enemy's
trenches.
(b)   Platoons are told off into three)reliefs as follows:-
                    No.1 Relief,   Sentry)
                    No. 2 Relief, Work.   )   1st. Relief.
                    No.3 Relief,   Sleep.)

                    No. 1 Relief, Work.   )
                    No.2 Relief,   Sleep.)   2nd. Relief
                    No.3 Relief,   Sentry.)

              No.1 Relief, Sleep.   )
              No. 2 Relief, Sentry.   )
              No.3 Relief, Work.   )   3rd Relief.
This method is adopted when work must be carried out at night and ensures
that all men perform the same proportion of duty throughout the night and
that the men for sentry always get an hour's sleep before going on sentry
duty.

          When trenches are very close and attack is expected, or the trench
so situated that it might be rushed, Platoons are told off into two reliefs
              No.1 Relief, Sentry
              No. 2 Relief, Sleep.
          When trenches are 200 yds. or more apart and there is little
work to do, 1/3 of the Platoon is on Sentry and 2/3 Sleep, giving each
man 1 hour as Sentry and 2 hours asleep.
          By day one Sentry is posted to every Section - 10 men - giving
1 hour on duty and 9 off, unless circumstances demand otherwise.

(c)   Sleeping on Post, Drunkenness or Insubordination. Immediately
confined in the Guard Detention Room, usually situated at Battn. Hqrs.

(d)   Every offence committed in the trenches is investigated by the
Company Commander who must remand the accused for disposal by the C. O.
          As far as applicable, cases are disposed of by the C. O. in
accordance with para 493, K.R. and the Army Act.
          For all offences mentioned in (c), N. C. O.'s and men are remand
- ded for Courts Martial.

(e)   In accordance with R. P., 14 (a) (b). R. P. (4) C. D. E.

(f)   In accordance with R. P. 13 and advised to plead " Not Guilty"
and either to make a verbal statement in his own defence, or hand in a
written statement.

(g)   Entirely responsible for the Clothing, Equipment, Discipline,
Organization, Interior Economy and training of the Platoon to his
Company Commander.

(h)   No man is allowed to fall out without written permission from an
Officer. An Officer is always detailed to march in rear of the Battalion
or Company to take the names of all men who fall out.
          The Medical Officer marches in rear and attends to the sick.
          Any man who falls out without permission is severly dealt with.

(i)(1) By means of Battalion Orders.
     (2) No man is allowed to quit the trench without written permission,
or in charge of an N. C. O.
(j)   Transport Officer and Quartermaster are responsible to the C.O.

(k)   When possible, all rations are cooked in rear and carried up by
Fatigue parties supplied by the Company in Support, or Battalion in reserve
(if any.)
          Usualy brought to a point of safety (a) in 1st. Line Transport
with muffled wheels, (b) Pack Animals.
          Pack animals are considered the best method, especially if
suitable bags and panniers could be provided as there is very little noise
caused by the Mules.

(1)   The Water Carts are under the direct supervision of the Medical
Officer and the filling of these is done by the R. A. M. C. water duty men
under his charge.
          The carts are brought up as near to the trenches as possible
and a Guard put on them. No man is allowed to use water other than that
from the carts, unless any spring or other water supply passed by the
Medical Officer as fit for use.
          One man per section is detailed to fill and collect Water bottles
for his section twice daily and the party from each Company is conducted
to the Water Carts by an N. C. O.
(m)
          All ranks are always in possession of their Gas Helmets and

(m)   All ranks are always in possession of their Gas Helmets and Respirators which are inspected twice weekly.
       When in Trenches, everyone is warned of the approach of Gas either (a) Gongs (b) Whistle (c) 3 "g,s" on a bugle and everyone stands to.
       The Bugle (As practised by the 1st. Division) is considered the best and quickest warning as it can be easily heard and picked up by Bugles and Units on right, left and rear.

(n)   RIFLES. At 9a.m. and 6p.m. daily.
       AMMUNITION. Immediately after wet weather . During the day each man's rounds are checked to see if he has the proper number prior to evening. " stand to ".
       KITS. Inspected on the 2nd day after return from the trenches and completed as far as possible during the rest period.

(o)   When in Billets, the Kit is always sent with the man.
       In trenches, Ordinary cases . Kits are sent with the man. If wounded as soon as possible according to circumstances.
       During an engagement. Practically impossible except in cases of men who are slightly wounded and who take their Kits with them.

(p)   Parties commanded by an Officer, by the Adjutant.
       Small parties by the Regtl. Sergt. Major.
       All parties are taken in proportion to the strength of Coy's.

(q)   Part 1 Orders are published daily in accordance with regulations, dealing with Discipline, Organisation, Interior Economy and Administration.
       Part 2 Orders, which deal with Promotions and Appointments ,Pay, Transfers, Discharges , Deaths and Invaliding home of all ranks, are published by the D. A. G. 3rd. Echelon, from A. F. B. 213, forwarded every Sunday.
       The above orders are in type and are read out to Platoons at 7a.m. daily. They are then hung up on a notice board for the men's perusal, also Intelligence Summaries and all matters affecting the men.

(r)   (1) Drawn and issued much in the same manner as rations.
       Braziers are usually taken over as Trench Stores and are distributed to Platoons and Officers according to strength.
       (2) Very few have had any experience with the distribution of Braziers.

(s)   Duty of the Transport Officer. Periodical Inspections are held by the C. O.

(t)   Battalion Medical Officer entirely responsible. He has 1 Cpl and 4 men of the R. A. M. C. placed at his disposal for the care and protection of water only.

(u)   Sanitary arrangements are inspected twice daily by the M. O. and Battn. Sanitary Squad, consisting of 1 Sergt. and 8 men.
       Latrines, Refuse Pits, Incinerators, Grease Traps etc. are arranged by the M. O. in conjunction with O.C. Coys.
       Buckets are better than earth latrines as they can be removed and the contents buried at night.
       A good supply of Chloride of Lime and Creasol is necessary and should be kept as trench stores.
       Fire Trenches and Dug-Outs are inspected after meals and no meat, bread etc. is allowed to be trodden into the ground.

(v)   (a) Taught by Platoon Commanders and N. C. O,s when the Battalion is resting in Billets.
       (b) (1) Safety catches are always kept raised . Any man found (at any time) other than when firing with the safety catch down is severly punished.
       (2) No man is ever allowed to place his hands over muzzle of rifle at any time.
       (3) Whenever the trigger is pressed, the muzzle must be pointing upwards. (During cleaning of arms.)

(w)

(w) (a) Food is protected from flies according to the material at hand. When possible, the meat wrappers are washed and used for this purpose.
(b) Incinerators and Refuse Pits are constructed for all refuse, tins etc.

SPECIAL NOTE.

(a)   It is suggested that all men awarded 56 days detention or more, should be taken from the Unit and handed to the A. P. M. for Work on Defences.
    It is a very difficult duty for the Battalion to carry out when in fire trenches and billets as they are always other prisoners undergoing sentence awarded by the C. O., up to 28 days and other men confined awaiting trial and Promulgation of Sentence.
    Guard Detention Rooms are not available in Fire Trenches

(b)   It is also suggested that clerical duties be reduced to a minimum while in Fire Trenches.
    As a rule there is only a small damp "Dug - out" in which to carry out these duties and the amount of clerical work at present carried out, which arrives from many other sources other than the Brigade or Division, keeps an Adjutant hard at work from 8a.m. to 10 p.m. daily, giving this Officer practically no time to attend to the more serious duties of Organization and Supervision of the Fire Trenches.

(Sgd.) J. S. Stewart. Lieut. Col.,
21/8/15.   Commanding 1/6th. A. &. S. Highrs.

WO 95/2865(1)

 PUBLIC RECORD OFFICE

document(s), being a map of the La Boiselle sector occupied by the 6th Btn. Argyll & Sutherland Highlanders, August 1915

has been removed to the Map Room, reference: MFQ 1251(1)

Date: 22rd August 1991   Signed: [signature]

"A" Form. **MESSAGES AND SIGNALS.** Army Form C. 2121.

No. of Message

This message is on a/c of: **APPENDIX IV**

TO	152ND INF BDE

Sender's Number	Day of Month	In reply to Number	AAA
694	25th		

Progress Report AAA. Operations AAA left Company AAA at 4.30pm enemy fired five heavy mortar bombs and several small bombs damaging one of our mortar emplacements AAA artillery retaliation obtained and also replied by mortar bombs on enemy's mortar emplacements AAA no further activity till 6pm when enemy renewed mortar bombardment AAA caused some damage to our trenches at 9.30pm enemy fired 3 torpedoes to vicinity of our working parties AAA arranged for reply by our mortars on enemy support trenches AAA no

From
Place
Time

"A" Form. — MESSAGES AND SIGNALS. — Army Form C. 2121.

further	activity	till	11	pm
when	enemy	fired	torpedo	to
save	place	AAA	Between	12
and	2am	trench	mortar	bombs
and	one	torpedo.	AAA	Our
mortars	are	outranged	by	enemy
torpedoes	which	are	much	heavier
than	our	bombs	AAA	
Centre	Company	AAA.	Quiet	night
AAA	no	mortars	or	grenades
AAA	Few	bursts	of	rapid
fire	but	ineffective.		
Right	Company	AAA.	Our	howitzers
registered	on	sap	at	461
yesterday	morning.	AAA	Rifle	fire
from	enemy	quiet	all	day
AAA	Snipers	only	active	after

"A" Form. — MESSAGES AND SIGNALS. — Army Form C. 2121.

dusk AAA Party working at sap at 461 fired on God by over artillery and infantry

Information AAA 9pm to 10pm enemy working party heard behind crater on left flank AAA little progress spotted on extension of sap at 461 AAA Machine Gun Report. AAA Two guns firing on heads of horse shoe sap AAA German working party reported ~~~~ ~~~~ 9.30pm AAA One gun traversed enemy's trench from left of 463 to 462 AAA

"A" Form. Army Form C. 2121.
MESSAGES AND SIGNALS.

Snipers Report AAA Sniping generally at loopholes a emplacements AAA German reported sniper at 456 while cleaning our lines AAA

From: 6th Argylls
Time: 8.30 a.m.

Appendix V.

STRENGTH RETURN MADE UP TO 12 NOON SATURDAY............................1915.

51st DIVISION.

UNIT.	(i.) Fighting strength for previous week, compiled in accordance with A.G.s instructions.		(ii.) Increase during week, due to drafts, etc., taken on strength of unit.		(iii.) Totals from (i.) and (ii.).		(iv.) Decrease during week–Casualties, etc., deducted from strength of unit.		"A." Fighting Strength compiled in accordance with A.G.s instructions.		"B." Details. (Included in "A").		REMARKS. (Brief notes regarding (iii), (iv) and "B", etc.).
	Officers.	O.R.	Officers.	O.R.	Officers.	O.R.	Officers.	O.R.	Officers.	O.R.	Officers.	O.R.	
6th August, 1915.	28	792	3	9 *Returned from Hospital*	31	801	1	17	30	784	–	20.	
13th " "	30	784	–	18	30	802	–	12	30	790	2	36.	
20th " "	30	790	–	34	30	824	1	11	29	813	3	65.	
27th " "	29	813	3	–	32	813	4	19	28	794	1	63.	
TOTALS													

Original Document descriptive of Trenches handed over by French at THIEPVAL.

Consignes

Under trench 141 Park 2ͤ Bataillon

Description and occupation of the Sector

It understands the front, starting from the road of Thiepval inclusively, to the North sape exclusively.

It is strong of 3 companies, having each 4 sections in the front line, to know.

1ͤʳ Company: From the road of Thiepval included to the second sentry post, south of the grey house, sape, excluded.

2ͤ Company: From that last point included to the North extremity of the "boyau Simon" included.

3ͤ Company: From the extremity North of the "boyau Simon" excluded to the extremity North of the Guyonvarch's trench.

In French liaison means direct communication, from company to bataillon, sections to company etc.

Liaison: To the right, to the Thiepval road with the first bataillon (Hill 141) to the left, to the North sape, with the third bataillon (wood).

Reserve: The fourth company, at the disposition of the chief of Bataillon, occupy the shelters in the little pine wood, others shelters for that company are to be finished, doors at the bottom of the Hill, North of the pine wood or in the ground (south part) of the way, that leads to the Park Kitchens.

In the meantime, the sections that have no shelters, of the reserve company, might be sheltered, either on the North part of Aucreville, or in the reserve shelters of the park which are not occupied.

Duties in the trench (day time)

In principles, one third of the men are on duty (sentry), one third rest themselves in the shelters, one third works in the trench, brings food to the men, and do all kind of jobs.

The company in reserve carries all the material such as wood, wire iron, etc.

Night Duties

During the night half the men are on duty — one chief of section is on duty permanently in the trench during the night, his attentions must be great, as regards to the vigilance of the sentries in the ports in front of the trench, called (poste d'écoute) and also when the patrouilles are going out or coming back in the trench.

The Captains and the chief of Bataillon, must see to the execution of that duty

In case of alarm, all the men take quickly their places in the trench

Alimentation Underofficers and Men

There is kitchens for the second and third companies of the Park, in the ravin between the wood and the park. The Kitchens for the first and fourth companies are in Authuille (Rolling Kitchens)

Officers

There is in the Park, one Kitchen and one Dining room, about 10 or 12 couverts (companies II and III.

The officers of the first company, can send soldiers to take their meals from that kitchen and have them, with the captain, at his post for instance. Those of the fourth company, have theirs prepared at Authuille or for the present, in the park, while the buildings of the shelters are going on, near the pine wood trees

Drinking Water

Springs water on the banks of the river ancre to the west of the wood, the way to get to it, is the following: Compagnies II and III take the telephonic "boyau" way to the Kitchens "boyau" along the wood South-East, and south then the way along the west part of the wood, to the springs, recipients such as milkmen tinpots are in use for it, to carry water from the springs to the trench

The company I and IV take that itinirairy, through the boyau de Fontenay and the little pine wood

Washing water Hygiene

River ancre; dangerous point one has to avoid passing elsewhere, than in the ways dug out of the ground, specially towards the ravin of the river ancre, between the border south of

Cutting of Wood in the Park and Wood of Chiepval

the wood, to the little pine wood, which is seen from the hill 141, one has only to walk 200 yards away to the North or to the South near by the riverside and be quite safe. In principles it is forbidden, in both the Park and wood, there is danger of cutting too much for the defense, not only the big trees, but also the young shoots on the border, which hide so well our positions; but one can take the wood already fallen and dead for kitchens fires

Cutting of Wood special consign

Is reserved in Aveluy's wood (see special consigns) which says that men have to carry timber on their shoulders, at least from Authuille to the trench

II Consigns in case of attack

A. Compagnies: I, II, III must resist to the last extremity in the trench of first line, so that, to limit the success of the enemy on one point, by cutting out of the trench between sections and companies.

B. Company: IV (Reserve of the bataillon)

One section occupy the trench "Lamour", facing the Park half a section, the other half facing the trench "le Digabel".

One section occupy the trench "Le Corré" between the boyau de Fontenay and the road of Chipval

The other half of the company, is at the disposition of the captain, for counter-attack either in the ravin or going down the hill 141

III Help to Wounded

A Red cross post, is situated, near by the kitchens of the Park, is particularly for the use of the II and III companies, of the Park.

Actually the companies I and IV would send directly their wounded to Authuille

A Red cross post could be provided

or put up, for these, two companies on the wood pathway, behind the little pine wood.

Rolling stretchers from Ctuthville can come to that point

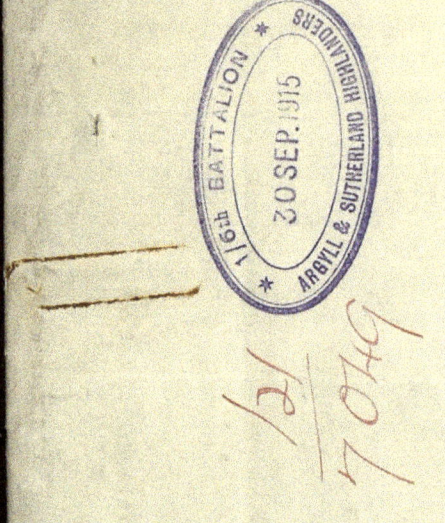

51st Division

121/7049

CONFIDENTIAL.

WAR DIARY OF 6th. BATTN. ARG. AND SUTH'D. HIGHRS.

From, 1/9/15... To, 30/9/15..

(Volume V)

CONFIDENTIAL
No. 134
152ⁿᵈ INF. BDE.

5N.

Volume VII
Army Form C. 2118.
Page 1.

WAR DIARY
or
~~INTELLIGENCE SUMMARY.~~
(Erase heading not required.)

1/6th Bn. Arg. y. Suthld. Highrs

Instructions regarding War Diaries and Intelligence Summaries are contained in F. S. Regs., Part II. and the Staff Manual respectively. Title pages will be prepared in manuscript.

Place	Date	Hour	Summary of Events and Information	Remarks and references to Appendices
LA BOISSELLE	1/9/15		Battalion in Fire Trenches. Battalion relieved in accordance with Bde. Operation Order No.14. Relief of C. Coy. commenced at 6.30 p.m. Remainder of Battalion relieved by 11 pm. Battalion proceeded independently by Companies to Billets at LAVIEVILLE arriving about 2 a.m.	
LAVIEVILLE	2/9/15		Battalion in Rest Billets. Cleaning and washing of clothing, equipment and person.	
"	3/9/15	11.45 a.m.	Battalion in Rest Billets. Working party 300 men under Capt. W.T. GILLESPIE detailed for work in Rear Trenches. Capt. Y. Adjt. A.G. THOMAS reported for duty from Leave.	
"	4/9/15		Battalion in Rest Billets. Working party 300 men under Captain H. McCHAFFIE for work on Rear Trenches	

Army Form C. 2118.

WAR DIARY
or
~~INTELLIGENCE SUMMARY~~
(Erase heading not required.)

1/6th Bn. A.& S. Highrs

Page 2.

Place	Date	Hour	Summary of Events and Information	Remarks and references to Appendices
LAVIEVILLE	5/9/15		Battalion in Rest Billets. Working party 150 men under Captain H. M^cHAFFIE supplied for work on Rear Trenches. Arrangements are being made to make LAVIEVILLE the Winter Quarters of the Battalion. A Committee, consisting of Major R. STEWART, Captain W.T. GILLESPIE, and Lieut. J.A.G. SHANKS was appointed by the C.O. to investigate and report on accommodation and repairs necessary in the village.	
"	6/9/15		Battalion in Rest Billets. Working parties (a) 150 under Captain J.H.G. SWAN. (b) 200 under Captain S. COATS supplied for work on Rear Trenches.	
"	7/9/15		Battalion in Rest Billets. Working party 300 strong under Captain W.T. GILLESPIE supplied for work on Rear Trenches. Test Alarm carried out by Battalion. Order received at 4.15 p.m.; Battalion ready to move 4.50 p.m.	

Army Form C. 2118.
Page 3.

WAR DIARY
or
~~INTELLIGENCE SUMMARY.~~
(Erase heading not required.)

1/6th Bn. Arg and Suthd. Highrs

Instructions regarding War Diaries and Intelligence Summaries are contained in F. S. Regs., Part II. and the Staff Manual respectively. Title pages will be prepared in manuscript.

Place	Date	Hour	Summary of Events and Information	Remarks and references to Appendices
LAVIEVILLE	8-9-15	—	Battalion in Rest Billets. Working party 300 under Capt. W. Gillespie supplied for work on rear trenches. Inspection of Transport and Machine Gun Section by C.O.	
"	9-9-15	—	Battalion in Rest Billets. Working party 150 under Capt. A. McAuffie supplied for work on rear trenches.	
"	10-9-15	—	Battalion in Rest Billets. Company inspections of clothing and kit.	
"	11-9-15	—	Battalion in Rest Billets. Orders received for Battalion to proceed to Fire Trenches. Battalion paraded in marching order at 5pm and proceeded to Fire Trenches 1/6th (E3) Section via ALBERT and ALBERT – LA BOISSELLE Road. Battalion relieved 7th. Black Watch about 9pm; all reliefs completed about 9.30pm. A few shells landed on LA BOISSELLE Road while relief was in progress but without doing any damage.	
1 Gt (E3) SECTOR	12-9-15		Battalion in Fire Trenches. Dispositions shown on sketch map attached. One platoon of A Coy. are situated in advanced trench within 20 yds. of German trenches. Lieut. Col. J.S. STEWART and Capt. J.H.C. SWAN admitted to hospital.	App. 1

Army Form C. 2118.

WAR DIARY
or
INTELLIGENCE SUMMARY
(Erase heading not required.)

1/6th Bn. A.Y.S. Highrs.

Page 4.

Place	Date	Hour	Summary of Events and Information	Remarks and references to Appendices
1 LOT(E3) SECTOR	13.9.15		Bombardment of A Coy's trenches by heavy mortar bombs. We have commenced to push forward a sap from the right portion of centre sector. Artillery and M.G. Fire lasting from 9.40 pm till 9.55 pm heard on our right.	
"	14.9.15		Enemy mine exploded in front of sector occupied by our right company. Dispositions of companies re-arranged as follows:- Right Coy. D, Centre Coy. A, Left Coy. B, In support C. Capt. H.K. Locke reported for duty from leave. Capt. A. Craig admitted to Hospital. Capt. W. Gillespie assumed command of C. Coy.	
"	15.9.15		Our Artillery sent over 10 H.E. shells into La Boisselle between 12.45 pm and 1.15 pm with good results. 10th Corps. Commander visited commander trenches	
"	16.9.15		Little activity on either side.	
"	17.9.15		Operation order ordering relief received. Battalion relieved by 8th Suffolks and proceeded to Rest Billets at Lavieville arriving about 12 midnight. Landscape sketch showing range of prominent objects in sector enclosed	App II

Army Form C. 2118.
Page 5.

16th Bn. A.T.S. Highrs.

WAR DIARY
~~INTELLIGENCE SUMMARY~~
(Erase heading not required.)

Instructions regarding War Diaries and Intelligence Summaries are contained in F.S. Regs., Part II and the Staff Manual respectively. Title pages will be prepared in manuscript.

Place	Date	Hour	Summary of Events and Information	Remarks and references to Appendices
LAVIEVILLE	18.9.15.		Battalion at rest. Cleaning of person, clothing and equipment.	
"	19.9.15	2.45pm	Battalion moved to new billeting area at SENLIS	
SENLIS	20.9.15		Battalion at rest. Working party 250 men supplied for work on third line defences, under Captain H.K. LOCKE. Operation Order received ordering relief.	
HÉNENCOURT	21.9.15	2.45pm	Battalion in Mass was inspected by the Secretary of State for War, Lord KITCHENER	
		3.15pm	Battalion proceeded by march route to reserve Billets at AVELUY arriving about	
AVELUY	21.9.15	7pm.	Battalion in Brigade Reserve. 630 rifles.	
AVELUY.	22.9.15		Battalion in Brigade Reserve. Numerous fatigue parties furnished.	
AVELUY	23.9.15		Fatigue parties furnished. 4 Officers and 250 other ranks furnished to Brigade for purpose of digging up to French instructions. Beneath our wire preparatory to attack	
AVELUY.	24.9.15		Fatigue parties furnished according to Brigade instructions. Lieut. W. SHANKS admitted to Hospital.	
"	25/9/15		Fatigue parties furnished. Lieut. B.M. ROBERTSON appointed Battn. Grenadier Officer. Regtl Grenadiers organised in accordance with "War Establishments", June, 1915. 2/Lieut. C. GARDNER appointed Assistant M.G. Officer.	
"	26/9/15		Lieut. A.M. CLEMENT admitted to hospital. Bulletins received showing the advance made by the Allies on the Western Front. Information received that attack	App.III

WAR DIARY
~~INTELLIGENCE SUMMARY~~
(Erase heading not required.)

Army Form C. 2118.

16th Bn. Q.O. Highrs

Page 6

Place	Date	Hour	Summary of Events and Information	Remarks and references to Appendices
AVELUY.	24/9/15	5 pm	by 1st. Army commenced at 6.30 a.m. 25th. and was progressing satisfactorily. Battalion in billets in Brigade Reserve relieved by 1/4th.Bn. Loyal North Lancs. Regt. and proceeded to temporary billets at MARTINSART. arriving about 6.30 pm. March was accomplished by platoon marching at 50 yds. interval. Casualties for period. 1 wounded.	
MARTINSART 24/9/15.			Cleaning of clothing and person. 2 patrols of 1 N.C.O. and 6 men each sent out at 9.30 p.m. on special duty in vicinity of MARTINSART. to look for suspected German spy. Each patrol under the command of an officer (Lieuts. L.L. SHEARER and C. GARDNER)	
"	28/9/15.	3.30 p.m.	Inspection of Battn. by G.O.C., 51st. (Highland) Division. New French maps of Sector received and issued to Headquarters and Companies. Maps received :— ALBERT (Combined Sheet) 1/40,000.; Sheet 67 D. S.E. 1 & 2 (Part of) 1/10000.; Sheet 57 d. S.E. 4. 1/1000.	
"	29/9/15	7.30 p.m	Operation Order No. 19 received ordering relief. Arrangements made for Battalion to proceed to Trenches at THIEPVAL on night of 30th. inst.	
"	30/9/15	9 a.m.	One officer per company bombing and sniping officers proceeded to Trenches to take over work in progress and familiarise themselves with defences etc. Battalion proceeded to Fire Trenches at THIEPVAL, relieving 7th. Royal Highrs. in sub-sector G.2.	

Army Form C. 2118.

Page. 7.

WAR DIARY
or
~~INTELLIGENCE SUMMARY~~
(Erase heading not required.)

1/6th Bn. A. & S.H.

Place	Date	Hour	Summary of Events and Information	Remarks and references to Appendices
MARTINSART	30.9.15	8.30 am	German aeroplane brought down just outside MARTINSART by British aeroplane turning machine gun fire on it. Enemy machine was wrecked. Both pilot and observer killed.	Int. Off.
			Casualties for September, 1915.	
			<table><tr><td></td><td>Officers</td><td>Others</td></tr><tr><td>Killed.</td><td>nil.</td><td>nil.</td></tr><tr><td>Wounded.</td><td>nil.</td><td>6.</td></tr><tr><td>Sick.</td><td>5.</td><td>93.</td></tr><tr><td>Rejoined for Duty.</td><td>nil.</td><td>64.</td></tr></table>	
			Summary of Weekly Strength States for month, enclosed.	App. IV.

R. Stewart MAJOR.
O.M.B.G. 1/6 ARG. & SUTH'D HIGH'rs

W A R D I A R Y

LIST OF APPENDICES.

    1 Sketch Map of ILOT Sector.

    2 Panoramic Sketch of ILOT Sector.

    3 Specimen Bulletin.

    4 Summary of Weekly Strength States.

WO 95/2865 (2) - (4)

PUBLIC RECORD OFFICE

document(s), being

(2) Map of La Boiselle showing infantry points, Sept. 1915

(3) British and German trench systems in Sector E3 Ilôt, 1915

(4) Panoramic sketch of the Ilôt sector, 1915

have been removed to the Map Room, reference: MFQ 1251 (2) - (4)

Date: 27th August 1991.   Signed: [signature]

51st (HIGHLAND) DIVISION.
INTELLIGENCE SUMMARY.

25 Sept 1915

The following is a short summary of the operations of the allied forces on the West, as far as known:-

1.   First British Army has advanced on roughly a 7,000 yard front South of LA BASSEE Canal, gaining on the right some 4,000 yards in depth of the enemy's line. The 47th (London) Division have captured 2 guns. The Indian Corps have captured MOULIN DU PIETRE E. of FAUQUISSART, and are advancing on HAUT POMMERAU.

2.   In the ARRAS sector, the 10th French Army has reached or crossed the enemy's first line on the whole front of attack. The 21st French Corps is progressing East of SOUCHEZ.

3.   In CHAMPAGNE the enemy's first line has been taken on the whole front (RHEIMS to VAILLY ?). At one point Cavalry have crossed the German lines.

4.   In the ARGONNE, North of MINACOURT, the French have reached MAISON DE CHAMPAGNE near which 2 squadrons have been put through. The advance further East has been carried to half way between PERTHES and TAHURE. At PERTHES the advance is about 1,000 yards, and at SOUAIN 2½ kilometres.

--++++++++++++++++++++++

Appendix H.

51st DIVISION.

STRENGTH RETURN MADE UP TO 12 NOON SATURDAY .... 1915.

	1. Fighting Strength for Previous Week		2. Increase during week due to Drafts etc.		3. Totals from (1) Y (11)		4. Increase Decrease during week - Casualties &c		"A" Fighting Strength		"B" Detail (Included in A)		REMARKS. Brief notes regarding (2),(4),and "B" etc.
	Officers	O.R.	Officers	O.R.	Officers	O.R.	Officers	O.R.	Officers	O.R.	Officers	O.R.	
4th. Sept., 1915.	28	794.	—	13	28	807	1	11	27	800.	2	77.	
11th. " "	27	800.	—	2	27	802	—	—	27	802	2	93.	
18th. " "	27	802	—	—	27	802	—	8	26	772	7	78.	
25th. " "	26	772	—	—	26	772	—	6	26	766	5	81.	

Note. Column "B" shows all men sick or in any way detached from Unit.

121/7384

6.N.
B.M.

51st Division

1/6th A.&S.H'rs.
Vol XL
Oct 15

CONFIDENTIAL.
No. 134
152nd INF. BDE.

CONFIDENTIAL.

WAR DIARY

of

1/6th. Battn. Arg. and Suth'd. Highrs.

From, 1st. Oct., 1915. To, 31st. Oct., 1915.

VOLUME VIII

Army Form C. 2118.

Volume VIII
Page 1.

WAR DIARY
or
~~INTELLIGENCE SUMMARY~~
(Erase heading not required.)

CONFIDENTIAL
No. 134.
1/2/4 INF. BDE.

16th Bn. A.S.H.

Instructions regarding War Diaries and Intelligence Summaries are contained in F. S. Regs, Part II. and the Staff Manual respectively. Title pages will be prepared in manuscript.

Place	Date	Hour	Summary of Events and Information	Remarks and references to Appendices
THIEPVAL (Sub Sector G.2)	1/10/15		Battalion in Fire Trenches. Companies distributed as follows:- Right: A Coy.; Centre, C. Coy.; Left, D. Coy.; Support, B. Coy. and Details. Approximate numbers in Fire Trench. 414; in Support 188. Reliefs completed in good order with 2 casualties. Quiet night. Dry, cold starlit night with no moon visible.	APP. 1.
"	2/10/15		Battalion in Fire Trenches. Situation generally quiet during the day. In the afternoon German Trench Mortars became more active near point 462. 3 large bombs and 3 smaller ones were landed in front of fire trench. Artillery retaliation asked for and obtained 3 to 5 minutes later in the form of 4 H.E. Shells, two of which failed to explode. Lieut. Col. STEWART, J.S. invalided to England. (Base Part. II Order, 131, of 30/9/15) as from 23/9/15.	
"	3/10/15		Battalion in Fire Trenches. Situation quiet. No. 1358 Pte. J. Wilson shot accidentally while on sentry duty.	

WAR DIARY or INTELLIGENCE SUMMARY

Army Form C. 2118.

16th Bn. A.I.F. Hughes

No. 134.
152nd INF. BDE.

Page 2.

Place	Date	Hour	Summary of Events and Information	Remarks and references to Appendices
THIEPVAL (G.2. Sector)	4/10/15		Battalion in Fire Trenches. Draft of 10 Officers and 17 other ranks arrived from Base. Name of Officer, 2nd. Lieut. J. RITCHIE. Posted to 'A' Coy.	
"	5/10/15		Battalion in Fire Trenches. Situation quiet. Heavy rainfalling damaging trenches in parts of sub-sector.	
		4:30pm.	20 yds. of 'C' Coy. trench blown in by trench mortar from 402. Howitzer retaliated. Repairs in progress.	
"	6/10/15		Battalion in Fire Trenches. Situation quiet. Repair of trenches continues.	
		10pm.	Enemy working parties out in front repairing wire at 404, dispersed by machine-gun fire.	
"	7/10/15		Battalion in Fire Trenches. Weather cold and dry. Wind calm S.E.	
		12.10pm	Enemy working party seen at point 50 yds. right of 396. Machine gun, rifle and artillery fire opened causing cessation of work. This was resumed and continued as opportunity offered during the day. Enemy working parties have been active all day. Am trying to discover reason for this.	

WAR DIARY or **INTELLIGENCE SUMMARY**

1/6th A.Y.S.H.

No. 134.

152nd INF. BDE.

Page 3

Place	Date	Hour	Summary of Events and Information	Remarks and references to Appendices
THIEPVAL. Sub-sector G.2.	5/10/15		Battalion in Fire Trenches. Situation quiet during the daylight. Between 5 p.m. and 12 midnight enemy bombarded and caused considerable damage in vicinity of fire trenches at 153. Sap No.10, SAUCHIEHALL STREET (30 yds) and several dug-outs completely blown-in, also part of WORGAN STREET and 10 yards of parapet in Fire Trench near Sap No.10. 4 men buried, were recovered at daybreak, dead. 1 man severely wounded in the head, not expected to live. 5 others buried but were dug out during the night. 1 man arm broken, several sprains. 15 others to Hospital suffering from shock. H.E. Shells fired from short range with a retarded fuse were used. Enemy's objective would appear to be our West Bomb Thrower evidently located by him. Wire in front of Sap 10 badly damaged. Working parties at once commenced digging out the buried men and a party of the 5th. Seaforths did good work in this respect during the night.	

Army Form C.2118.

WAR DIARY
or
~~INTELLIGENCE SUMMARY.~~

(Erase heading not required.)

CONFIDENTIAL
No. 134
No. 152nd INF. BDE.

1/6th Battn. A.&S.H.

Page IV

Instructions regarding War Diaries and Intelligence Summaries are contained in F.S. Regs., Part II. and the Staff Manual respectively. Title pages will be prepared in manuscript.

Place	Date	Hour	Summary of Events and Information	Remarks and references to Appendices
THIEPVAL G.2. Sector	9/10/15		Battalion in Fire Trenches. Situation quiet. Operation Order No. 20 received ordering relief	
	10/10/15		Battalion in Fire Trenches. Situation quiet during daylight. About 1.30 pm. heavy cannonade was heard on our right about 20 mile S.E. apparently.	
		About 5.30 pm	every contested sub-sector G.1. and our right coy. with heavy mortars. This continued during part of the period of relief which commenced about 6.30 pm.	
		6.30 pm	Battalion relieved in Fire Trenches by 1/7th. Gordon Highrs. Proceeded to rest	
		9 pm	Billets at MARTINSART, arriving between the hours of 9 pm and 11 pm. Companies marched back independently by platoons at 40 yds interval. 1 men wounded.	
MARTINSART.	11/10/15		Battalion in Rest Billets. Cleaning and washing. Rifle and kit inspections.	
	12/10/15		Battalion in Rest Billets. Cleaning frt. washing &c	
	13/10/15		Battalion in Rest Billets. Working party 150 men under Captain Coats found for work in G.2. Sector. 2 men wounded. Captain S. COATS proceeded on leave.	
	14/10/15		Battalion in Rest Billets. Route march. 3465 L.Cpl. W. Muir, Captain W. GILLESPIE and Captain J.H. BROWN recommended for awards for acts of gallantry.	App. 2

CONFIDENTIAL
No. 134.
152nd INF. BDE.

Army Form C. 2118.

WAR DIARY
~~INTELLIGENCE SUMMARY~~
1/6th Bn. A.I.S.H.

Page V

(Erase heading not required.)

Instructions regarding War Diaries and Intelligence Summaries are contained in F. S. Regs., Part II. and the Staff Manual respectively. Title pages will be prepared in manuscript.

Place	Date	Hour	Summary of Events and Information	Remarks and references to Appendices
MARTINSART	15/10/15		Battalion in Rest Billets. Working party 150 strong supplied for work in G. Sector.	
		10.23pm	Alarm signal given by wire from Brigade Headquarters. Battalion turned out on alarm post ready to move by 10.40pm. Horse for M.G. Limbers not however booked in. Battalion dismissed from Alarm Post by 11.7pm. 10.30pm	
"	16/10/15		Battalion in Rest Billets. Tactical exercise carried out near ENGLEBELMER according to prearranged scheme.	
"	17/10/15		Battalion in Rest Billets. Divine Service.	
"	18/10/15		Battalion in Rest Billets. Tactical schemes carried out by companies in vicinity of ENGLEBELMER.	
"	19/10/15		Battalion in Rest Billets. Fatigue parties (250 men in all) supplied for work on bomb proof shelters in G2 Sector in accordance with 51st Div. Circular Memorandum No. 23.	
		8.30pm	Operation Order No. 21, received ordering relief for 20th inst.	

1577 Wt. W10791/1773 500,000 1/15 D.D. & L. A.D.S.S./Forms/C. 2118.

WAR DIARY or INTELLIGENCE SUMMARY

Army Form C. 2118.

1/6th Bn. A.I.S.A.

CONFIDENTIAL No. 134
162nd INF. BDE.

Page 6

Place	Date	Hour	Summary of Events and Information	Remarks and references to Appendices
MARTINSART	20/10/15		Battalion in Rest Billets. Fatigue parties (250 men in all) supplied for work on bomb-proof shelters in G.2. Sector. Orders for move to AUTHUILLE issued to companies etc.	
		6pm	Battalion moved off independently by companies to take over defences at AUTHUILLE as Battalion in Brigade reserve. Sketch plan of defences enclosed. Major R.I. RAWSON, Gloucestershire Regt; arrives to assume command of the Battalion.	APP 4
AUTHUILLE	21/10/15		Battalion in Rest Billets. Brigade Reserve. Working parties supplied for work in defences. Laying wire, etc.	
"	22/10/15		Battalion in Brigade Reserve. Working parties supplied for work on defences, laying wire etc.	
"	23/10/15		Battalion in Brigade Reserve. Working parties supplied for work on defences, laying wire etc.	
"	24/10/15		Battalion in Brigade Reserve. Working parties supplied for work on defences.	
"	25/10/15		" " " " " " " " " " "	
"	26/10/15		" " " " " " " " " " "	
"	27/10/15		" " " " " " " " " " "	

CONFIDENTIAL
No. 134.
152nd INF. BDE.

WAR DIARY

Army Form C. 2118.

1/6th Bn. A.Y. & S. Highrs   Page 7.

Place	Date	Hour	Summary of Events and Information	Remarks and references to Appendices
AUTHUILLE	28/10/15		Battalion in Brigade Reserve. Working parties supplied for work on defences.	
"	29/10/15		" " " " " " " " " " " " " " " "	
"	30/10/15		" " " " " " " " " " " Operation Order No 22 received ordering relief to take place. Battalion relieved by 1/6th. 13 Lack Watch at 6.45 pm. Companies marched off independently, 50 yards between platoons, to long	
"			over billets at Millencourt.	
MILLENCOURT	31/10/15		Battalion in Rest Billets. Washing and general cleaning up of person, clothing and equipment. Summary of Weekly Strength States enclosed. Casualties for month: 5 killed, 24 wounded.	Appx. IV

M Mann
LIEUT.-COL.
CMDG. 6TH ARG. & SUTHND HIGHRS

CONFIDENTIAL
No. 134.
No 2 INF. BDE.

LIST OF APPENDICES.

APPENDIX I   Sketch Plan of Sub-Sector G.2.
APPENDIX II   Recommendations for Awards.
APPENDIX III Sketch Plan of AUTHUILLE Defences.
APPENDIX IV   Summary of Weekly Strength States.

WO 95/2865 (5)

PUBLIC RECORD OFFICE

document(s), being a map of Sub Sector G2 — Thiepval, October 1915

has been removed to the Map Room, reference: MFQ 1251(5)

Date: 27th August 1991   Signed: William J.

appendix II

CONFIDENTIAL.
CONFIDENTIAL.

Headquarters,
~~Headquarters Infantry Brigade.~~
152nd. Infantry Brigade.

I forward herewith recommendation for the Distinguished Conduct Medal for No. 3456, L/Cpl. Willial Muir of the Battn. under my Command for Gallant Conduct during the night of 8/9th October, 1915 when the Fire Trenches held by this unit were being bombarded by the enemy's Trench Mortars, details of which have already been fully reported.

I forward also, recommendations for Captain W.GILLESPIE and Captain J.H.Brown, Coy. Commander and Coy. Second in Command respectively for coolness and courage displayed during the bombardment.

Immediately the Sap was blown in Captain and Adjutant A.G Thomas went forward and inspected the damage and reported to me that it would be impossible to get the buried men out before day-break and then supervised the clearing of SAUCHIE-HALL STREET which had been blown in/for 30 yds.

Captain Thomas informed me that the Coy. was cool and collected (Although 20 men had been sent to Hospital) due to the coolness displayed by Captains Gillespie and Brown- which was noticed by myself when I went to the "Blown in" Trench I consider that the coolness displayed by these officers is worthy of the award for which I have the honour to recommend them.

Major,
14th. October, 1915.   Commanding, 1/6th. A. & S. H

CONFIDENTIAL
No. 134.
Army Form. W. 3121.

...152nd Infantry..Brigade. ...5/24..Division. ...10th..Corps.

Schedule No. (to be left blank.)	Unit.	Regtl. No.	Rank & Name.	Action for which commended.	Recommended by.	Honour or Reward.	Corps Register No.
	1/6th. Battn. Arg. & Suth'd. Highrs.	3456.	Lance Corporal. Muir, William.	Gallant conduct on the 8/9th Oct. 1915 when the Fire Trench was heavily bombarded by enemy Trench Mortars. Early in the bombardment about 5-30 p.m. a Tunnelled Listening Sap was blown in not far from the point of junction with Fire Trench. Communication was cut off, four men were on duty in the Sap, and it was necessary to ascertain whether the men had been killed or buried. L/Cpl. Muir volunteered to go over the parapet and through the wire entanglement into the Shell Hole. He returned by same route and reported that two men were suffering from shock whom he brought in and two men were buried. L/Cpl. Muir again went out accompanied by Captain J.H. Brown and commenced	Captain W. Gillespie. Captain J.H. Brown.	Distinguished Conduct Medal. (immediate)

[Stamp: 1/6th BATTALION, ARGYLL & SUTHERLAND HIGHLANDERS, 16 OCT 1915]

CONFIDENTIAL
No. 134
15/24 INF. BDE.

Army Form. W.3121.

.... Brigade. .... Division. .... Corps. .... { Corps Register No.

Schedule No. (to be left blank.)	Unit.	Regtl No.	Rank & Name.	Action for which	Recommended by.	Honour or Reward.
				digging out under fire the two buried men. They were exposed so much to rifle fire that a hasty parapet had to be built to protect them. Later about 10 p.m. a Dug-Out was blown in which held seven men, L/Cpl. Muir being one of the number. All the party were buried, two being instantly killed, L/Cpl. Muir dug himself out and then dug the first of remaining men out and although suffering from shock he was able to report to O.C. Coy. what had happened. This was the means of saving the lives of three more men. L/Cpl. Muir collapsed immediately after and had to be sent to Hospital.		

CONFIDENTIAL.
No. 134. Army Form. W. 3121.
152nd INF. BDE.

................Brigade. ....Division. ....Corps. .... Corps Register No.

Schedule No. (to be left Blank.)	Unit.	Regtl. No.	Rank & Name.	Action for which commended.	Recommended by.	Honour or Reward.
	1/6th. Battn. Arg. & Suth'd. Highrs.		Captain Gillespie, William.	Cool conduct and devotion to duty during the heavy bombardment of Fire Trenches 8/9th October 1915 by enemy Trench Mortars. 9 men being buried of whom 5 were dug out and their lives saved, 11 others being injured and suffering from shock. The calmness displayed by these Officers was reflected in the whole Company, and the work of rescue and repair to Trenches was carried out with regularity and expedition under rifle fire.	Major Stewart, R.	Military Cross.
			Captain Brown, James Hardie.		Captain & Adjutant A.G. Thomas.	

WO 95/2865 (5)

PUBLIC RECORD OFFICE

document(s), being a

sketch plan of Authuille showing its defences, October 1915

has been removed to the Map Room, reference: MFQ 1251 (6)

Date: 27th August 1991   Signed: [signature]

CONFIDENTIAL
No. 134.

Division _____ 152nd INF. BDE.

Strengths Return made up to 12 noon Saturday _____ 1915.

Unit.	(1) Fighting strength of field week completed again in accordance with O.R.'s instructions		(2) Increase during week due to drafts etc. taken in strength of units.		(3) Totals from (1) and (2)		(4) Decrease during week - casualties to deducted from strength of units		"A" Fighting Strength of unit completed in accordance with O.R.'s instructions		"B" Details (Included in "A").		Remarks. (Brief notes regarding (4) (A) Band "B" etc.)
	Officers	O.R.	Officers	O.R.	Officers	O.R.	Offrs.	O.R.	Offrs.	O.R.	Offrs.	O.R.	
2/10/15	26	766	—	—	26	766	—	14	26	752	6	57	
9/10/15	26	737*	1	17	27	754	1	14	26	740	6	57	*Men struck off under Bde. Orr.
16/10/15	26	740	—	—	26	740	—	21	26	719	6	73	
23/10/15	26	719	2	14	28	733	1	22	27	711	6	76	
30/10/15	27	711	—	1	27	712	1	18	27	694	6	74	
Totals													

APPENDIX IV

51st Division

152nd Inf. Bde.

CONFIDENTIAL
No. 134

D/7636

J.N.

CONFIDENTIAL.

WAR DIARY

of

1/6th. Battalion Argyll and Sutherland Highlanders.

FROM, 1st. Nov., 1915. TO, 30th. Nov. 1915.

VOLUME IX. Vol VII

WAR DIARY or INTELLIGENCE SUMMARY

Army Form C. 2118.

16th A.V.S.H.
152nd INF. BDE.
Volume IX
No. 134
Page 1.

Place	Date	Hour	Summary of Events and Information	Remarks and references to Appendices
MILLENCOURT	1/11/15	—	Battalion in Rest Billets. Inspection of M.G. Section by C.O.	
"	2/11/15	—	Battalion in Rest Billets. Working parties furnished for work on defences.	
"	3/11/15	—	Battalion in Rest Billets. Official intimation received that 3456, Lance Corporal William Muir, C. Coy. has been awarded the Distinguished Conduct Medal "For gallantly volunteering to go over the parapet into a listening sap that had been blown in by the enemy and bringing in men suffering from shock". This is the first award of this medal in the Brigade.	
"	4/11/15	—	Battalion in Rest Billets. Working parties furnished for work on defence.	
"	5/11/15	—	Battalion in Rest Billets. Company training under company officers, winter clothing, including sheepskin coats received.	
"	6/11/15	—	Battalion in Rest Billets. Arrangements in case of alarm revised.	
"	7/11/15	—	Battalion in Rest Billets. Operation order ordering relief. 1pm. Battalion proceeded via ALBERT to take over fire trenches in Sub-Sector F1. Trenches taken over and relief completed by 6pm. (Reference: Trench Map, 1/10,000. 57D. S.E. Sheet 4). Battalion on Right, 10th Essex Regt, 23rd, 13de., 18th Division. Battalion on Left, 6th Seaforth Highrs.	APP. I

Sub-sector
F1 (ONSLOW)

WAR DIARY

1/6th Bn. A.&S. Highrs.

Army Form C. 2118.

Page 2.

No. 134
132nd Inf. BDE.

Place	Date	Hour	Summary of Events and Information	Remarks and references to Appendices
Sub-sector F.1 (Courcelles)	8/11/15		Battalion in Fire Trenches. Situation quiet all day. Men employed in repair and improvement of trenches. Weather cold but dry. Very heavy rain during the night causing trenches to become very muddy.	
"	9/11/15		Battalion in Fire Trenches. Weather very wet and trenches muddy. Men employed in repair of trenches generally.	
"	10/11/15		Battalion in Fire Trenches. Weather wet; trenches muddy. Situation generally quiet.	
"	11/11/15		Battalion in Fire Trenches. Weather wet; trenches muddy. Situation generally quiet. Patrols going out, instructed to obtain, if possible, specimens of German barbed wire.	
"	12/11/15		Battalion in Fire Trenches. 2/Lieut. A. Lang joined Battalion from Base Depot. Portions of trench exceedingly dirty and the shelters are very leaky and in some instances dangerous. About 5 p.m. a shelter in C. Coy's portion of line collapsed and the beams in falling killed one man.	
"	13/11/15		Battalion in Fire Trenches. Situation quiet.	
"	14/11/15	1.30 p.m.	Battalion relieved in Fire Trenches by 8th A.&S.H. and proceeded independently by companies as relieved to Billets in Brigade Reserve at AVELUY.	

Army Form C. 2118.

1/6th Bn A.&S.H.

Page 3

WAR DIARY
or
INTELLIGENCE SUMMARY.
(Erase heading not required.)

CONFIDENTIAL
No. 134
/52nd INF. BDE.

Place	Date	Hour	Summary of Events and Information	Remarks and references to Appendices
AVELUY	14/4/16		2/Lieut. J.M. CALDWELL joined Battalion for duty from Base Depot, Etaples. Lieut. Col. R.I. RAWSON proceeded on leave to England from 15th till 22nd inst., Major R. STEWART assuming command of the Battalion during his absence. Specimen progress reports enclosed covering periods in trenches. Battalion in Brigade Reserve. Working parties supplied for work in F.L. Sector.	Appx I
"	15/4/16		Battalion in Brigade Reserve. Working parties supplied for work on F.L. Sector.	
"	16/4/16		Battalion in Brigade Reserve. Captain W. GILLESPIE admitted to Hospital sick.	
"	17/4/16		8 men sent to Base Depot for transfer to Home Establishment as munition workers.	
"	18/4/16		Battalion in Brigade Reserve. Working parties supplied for work on F.L. Sector.	
"	19/4/16	4.30 am	Battalion in Brigade Reserve. Order for "Practice Alarm" received. Battalion turned out on Alarm Post to await orders.	Appx II
"	20/4/16		Battalion in Brigade Reserve. Working parties supplied for work on F.L. Sector	
"	21/4/16		" " " " " " " " " "	
"	22/4/16		Battalion relieved by 1/7th. Royal Highrs. Relief commenced 8 pm. Companies proceeded independently to rest billets at HENENCOURT on completion of relief	

Army Form C. 2118.

WAR DIARY
or
INTELLIGENCE SUMMARY.
(Erase heading not required.)

1/6th A.V.S.R.

Page 4

CONFIDENTIAL
No. 134
152nd INF. BDE.

Place	Date	Hour	Summary of Events and Information	Remarks and references to Appendices
HENENCOURT	23/11/15		Battalion in Rest Billets. Kit inspection. Clearing of clothing from etc.	Shut Cutt
"	24/11/15		Battalion in Rest Billets. Arrangements made for action in case of alarm.	
"	25/11/15		Battalion in Rest Billets. Capt N.V. Capt, A.G. Thomson leave. Captain F.R. Lane acting adjutant.	
		10.45 p.m	Test Alarm. Battalion ready to move 10.50pm. On parade. 18 officers, 515 other ranks. 16 horses, 8 vehicles including two M.G. limbers	
"	26/11/15		Battalion in Rest Billets. 7 Officers, 318 Other ranks furnished for working parties in F. Sector.	Alek Cutt
"	27/11/15		Battalion in Rest Billets. Operation order received ordering relief for 28th inst.	Alek Cutt
"	28/11/15	2 pm	Battalion marched off independently by companies to take over trenches in G.2 sub-sector. Head of Battalion passed AUTHUILLE at 6pm. Battalion relieved 1/6th Liverpool Regt. Companies distributed from right left as follows A, B, D, Coys. C. Coy in support. In Fire Trenches, 354. other ranks. In support, 149 other ranks. Weather, dry, clear and frosty.	Alek Cutt
THIEPVAL G.2				
"	29/11/15		Battalion in Fire Trenches. Draft of 112 men arrived from Base 25/11/15.	
"	30/11/15		Battalion in Fire Trenches.	

WAR DIARY
or
~~INTELLIGENCE~~ SUMMARY. 1/6th. A.&.S.H.

(Erase heading not required.)

Army Form C. 2118.

Page 5

CONFIDENTIAL
No. 134
152nd INF. BDE.

Casualties for month:-

	Officers	Other Ranks
K	—	1
W	1 ×	1
M	—	—
TOTAL	1.	2.

× Lieut. D. N. Doyhrough.

Strength of Battalion during month.

Date.	(1) Fighting Strength last week		(2) Increase		(3) Total from (1) & (2)		(4) Decrease		(5) Fighting Strength		(6) Fighting not actually with Units	
	O.	O.R.	O.	O.R.	O.	O.R.	O.	O.R.	O.	O.R.	O.	O.R.
6/11/15	27	694	—	10	27	704	1	7	26	697	6	77
13/11/15	26	697	1	—	27	697	—	7	27	690	7	77
20/11/15	27	690	1	—	28	690	1	12	27	678	9	72
27/11/15	27	678	—	7	27	679	—	27	27	652	7	79

W Murrin
LIEUT-COL.
CMDG. 6TH ARG. & SUTHND HIGHRS

WO 95/2865(7)

 PUBLIC RECORD OFFICE

document(s), being

"Sketch Plan of F1 Sector Showing Artillery Points," Nov. 1915.

has been removed to the Map Room, reference: MFQ 1251(7)

Date: 27th August 1991   Signed: William J. T.

APPENDIX II

CONFIDENTIAL
No. 134
152 INF. BDE.

HEAD QUARTERS,
51st. (H) Division.

P.1.   6th. Arg. & Suth'd Highrs.

No enemy Artillery action on our front. Their Machine Guns have been less active during last 24 hours. Little rifle fire but large number of lights put up by them. At intervals during night fire was opened on German communication trench opposite 134 in co-operation with No. 4 M.G. It is doubtful if rifle or M.G. fire is effective as trench is very deep and well traversed. Just after dark enemy fired three rifle grenades which burst in rear of the trench. We retaliated with Rifle Grenades from No. 2 Sap. No. 1 M.G. firing from X.1.3.a.3.3. on enemy's communication trench and support trench on E of LA BOISSELLE. No. 2 Gun firing on enemy's trench at X.1.3. d.6.8. No. 4 Gun fired on road running through OVILLERS. Three German periscopes located and after fire by our snipers were withdrawn.

P.2.   5th. Seaforth Highrs.

Day passed without event and at night desultory rifle fire and short bursts of M.G. fire. Patrols were sent out but weather conditions were against effective observations and listening. One Patrol managed to reach enemy sap at X.1.a.3.8. going along track X.1.a.0.7. and in front of enemy barbed wire. Nothing was seen or heard but patrol reports strong heavy enemy wire on pickets 18" above ground. German T.M.Bomb came from about point X.1.a.7.8.

Supporting Points - 6th. Seaforth Highrs.

Artillery activity on both sides was hardly so pronounced as in the preceding period. Enemy artillery fired several shrapnel shells in the vicinity of LOWER DONNET, but there were not so many as on the previous day, and no damage was done. All traffic on the outside of LANCASTER AVENUE has been stopped and this may account for the fewer number of shells fired in this direction by the enemy. Enemy Machine Guns and Rifles were quiet, practically throughout the period.

(sgd) T.M.Booth, Major,
for Brigadier General,
Commdg. 152nd. Infantry Brigade.

10th. November, 1915.

2.

Officer Commanding,
1/5th Seaforth Highrs, 1/6th Argyll & Suth'd Highrs.
1/6th   do.   1/8th   do.

The above copy of summary of to-day's progress reports is forwarded for your information.

10th November 1915.

Major, Brigade Major,
152nd Infantry Brigade.

CONFIDENTIAL
No. 134

War Diary

152nd INF. BDE.

Head quarters,
51st. (H) Division.

MID-DAY REPORT.

P.1. **8th Arg. & Sutherland Highrs.**

Enemy Artillery inactive during the night. One shell only fired, over right of line. All quiet on front. Rifle fire kept up at intervals on German Communication trench 133/134 5-25 a.m. two Grenades burst in front of 132. No sign of new works on enemy lines. Following coloured lights observed, 11-15 p.m. red followed by white. 2 a.m. red, 4-30 a.m. red. Small part of trench in centre Coy's front has subsided. Repair in progress. No assistance required. Consider that facilities for observing enemy could be improved by making a continuation to listening post in 134 in a direction half left out to the edge of trench. Ground has been reconnoitered by patrol whose report confirms this view. Patrol also reported very little activity in German trenches. A few Germans seen on road near R 38,d 3/7. They appeared to drop into communication trench. Road now being watched. No.1. Gun firing on communication trenches N. of LA BOISELLE. No.2.Gun fired on OVILLERS. Two enemy M.G. retaliated at dusk but gave no trouble thereafter. Was unable to locate enemy guns. Gun behind WALTNEY STREET fired bursts at Sapg at point d24. Snipers have been on the alert and have gone some way to establish superiority over the Germans who have not been so active during last 24 hours. A German periscope appeared to have been smashed opposite point 135 and two others were withdrawn after our snipers had located them. Small German working party of about 4 men again located at R.1.b.4.8. and appeared to be deep- ing a trench. They only remained under observation for a short period. Three Germans observed this morning passing behind a ruined house in OVILLERS. One of them appeared to be carrying a heavy load. Spot was carefully watched but men did not come again under observation. Patrol from 134 under 2/Lt D.A.Brown out 6 P.M. returned 7.30 P.M. could find no German Sap. Reconnoitered dead ground in front of No.134. Near German wire, shell hole discovered with conical object stuck near its edge with leather handle, probably bomb disguised. Patrol under Lt. Forsyth out from 9 p.m. to 10.30 p.m. All quiet in front of 131/132. Our own wire also examined and required repair in six different places.

P.2. **5th Seaforth Highlanders.**

Enemy Artillery more active than usual except for heavy shells which landed about R.1.b.1.4. doing no damage. Enemy Field Guns fired at intervals into the wood. Enemy M.G. active during the night. One M.G. firing from about X.8.a.8.8. has the action of a Vickers Gun and is probably a captured Gun converted. A patrol went out to examine our barbed wire and to observe if enemy patrol were visiting our line. The wire in front of Right Company is in good condition and the ground in front was carefully patrolled but no sound of working parties was heard or enemy patrol seen.

Supporting Points/

(2)

CONFIDENTIAL
No. 134
152nd INF. BDE

Supporting Points - 6th Seaforth Highlanders.

At 7.30 a.m. an R.E. wagon and six horses came up the open by LANCASTER AV. to LOWER DONNET and shortly afterwards the enemy fired a salve of shrapnel at the R.E. dump LOWER DONNET. One engineer was wounded.

It is noted that *when* any large party congregated at LOWER DONNET dump the enemy shell this point, and it is probable they see from N.32.C.

Artillery activity normal. Machine Gun and rifle fire small.

(Signed) A. D. Thomson, Capt.
for Brigadier General
Commanding, 152nd. Infantry Brigade.

11th November, 1915.

Officer Commanding ,

~~1/5th Seaforth Highrs~~ ; 1/6th Argyll & Suth'd Highrs.
~~1/6th   do.~~   ; 1/8th   do.

For your information .

[signature] Thomson

Captain ,
Staff Captain ,
152nd Infantry Brigade.

11th November 1915 .

CONFIDENTIAL
No. 134
152nd INF. BDE.

Head Quarters
51st (H) Division

MID-DAY REPORT.

F.1.   6th Argyll & Sutherland Highrs.

Orders were issued to O.C.Coys.M.G. Officers and Intelligence Officer to keep a sharp lookout during the night and that bursts of M.G.Fire were to be kept up and Rifle Fire throughout the night. These instructions were carried out.

Reports received during night stated that there was little responce to our rifle and M.G. fire . The enemy's activity appeared to be normal. About 24 light shrapnel and 7 heavy Howitzers from direction of LA BOISSELLE were fired, mostly from direction of 135. No.1.M.G. fired on OVILLERS, No.2. on OVILLERS and trenches in front. No.3.Gun on communication trench.

No Patrols were sent out on account of the firing from our trenches. It is difficult to judge whether troops have been withdrawn from our front or not as there has been very little M.G. or rifle fire from the enemy during last three or four days and as far as can be ascertained the strength of the enemy in front remains the same. A Sentry and N.C.O. on duty reported enemy working party on their wire opposite 134 about 12-30 a.m. two Officers on the spot could however hear nothing .

F.2.   5th Seaforth Highrs .

Enemy Artillery action confined to sending over 3 or 4 small shells at intervals which did no damage. The majority landed in the wood near our right centre Coy. Patrols sent out and returned after period of patrolling and reported nothing unusual. Listening posts reported enemy working on barbed wire, opposite point 144 between 7 and 8 p.m. but owing to a patrol being out from our left Coy, fire could not be opened at once but on Patrol returning working party was dispersed by rifle fire. Heavy rifle and M.G. fire opened on enemy at intervals last night and this morning in order to draw enemy's fire and to ascertain if the enemy's trenches were strongly held or otherwise. Their rifle fire was normal but the M.G.'s fire rather more heavy than usual. It is thought that their front is held strongly by M.Gs. with comparatively few rifles. No.4.M.G. fired from position in CHEQUERBENT STREET at point 424, later traversing the cluster of trenches round that point. It is probable that during the day the enemy M.Gs are fixed on certain spots on our lines and fire single shots at intervals. Our Field Gun Battery supporting our Sector was tested last night with message test 143. It was sent from fire trench at 5-49p.m. What appears to be an enemy O.P. was located at X.2.d.1.5. but this needs to be verified. Several persons including apparently a Staff Officer were seen at this point making observations . They were fired on with the result that they approached with caution afterwards.

Supporting Points - 6th Seaforth Highlanders.

Artillery activity normal. There were several salvos of Shrapnel fired by the enemy at LOWER DONNET during the day but no damage was done. A few bursts of M.G. fire at night but otherwise quiet. At 7 a.m. a working party on RIVINGTON STREET & JOHN O'GAUNT STREET was evidently seen by the enemy. There was sniping and a M.G. was fired at the party. Just after the party was taken down from the parapet 3 salvos of Shrapnel were fired by the enemy. No damage was done. This party will in future work at night.

CONFIDENTIAL
No. 134
152nd INF. BDE.

(2)

Battn. in Brigade Reserve - 8th Argyll & Sth'd Hidrs.

Five shells fell in the vicinity of AVELUY at 3.45 p.m. on 11th. and a single shell fell somewhere near the village about mid-night. All the shells seem to come from THIEPVAL direction.

(Signed) T.M.Booth, Major,
Brigade Major.

For- Brigadier General,
Commanding 152nd Infantry Brigade.

12th, November, 1915.

Officer Commanding,

~~1/6th Seaforth Hgrs~~ , 1/6th Argyll & Suth'd Highrs.
~~1/6th do.~~ , 1/8th do.

Forwarded for your information.

T M Booth

Major,
Brigade-Major,
152nd Infantry Brigade.

12th November 1915.

War Diary

CONFIDENTIAL
No. 134
152nd INF. BDE.

Headquarters,
51st (Highland) Division.

PROGRESS REPORT.

P.1.   6th Arg. & Suth'd. Highrs.

Enemy artillery quiet during last 24 hours. Little M.G. or rifle fire, 1 M.G. firing during night on Sap 424.
Following lights seen:-
    9.15 P.M.   2 Red flares from LA BOISSELLE.
    9.25 P.M.   2 Green flares from direction of left of OVILLERS
    10.10 P.M.   2 red flares seen opposite P.2.
    4.45 A.M.   2 red flares
    5.25 A.M.   Red light followed by green.

German working heard opposite Point 133. Sentries opened fire in direction of noise.
No. 1 Gun fired on OVILLERS. No. 2 Gun on communication trenches N. of LA BOISSELLE.
Sniping carried on as usual. Gradually obtaining a superiority over the enemy.
About 3.30 P.M. what appeared to be a small engine with 5 trucks attached, also a motor wagon, were observed on road to right of OVILLERS. Range judged 2,000 yards. Several Germans with full packs observed leaving a trench in rear of fire trench and appeared to cut over fields and not proceed out of view by means of communication trench. Distance about 2,500 yards. Sniped at them but no result noticed. Snipers on right reported that several German bombs appeared to fall short among their own barbed wire near OVILLERS about 4 P.M.

P.2.   5th Bn. Seaforth Highlanders.

In retaliation to our Art. bombardment of yesterday, enemy replied with small shells on corner of Wood K.1.B.4.3. and others passed over in direction of AUTHUILLE. 3 shells made direct hits on trench at Point 143. Enemy's M.G. very active after dusk, and the whole sector was swept by the fire at short intervals until well into night. No. 4 M.G. started firing about 6 P.M. and drew fire of at least 2 enemy M.G.s. 1 Patrol sent out but returned shortly after owing to enemy firing on them. Another patrol went out at 2 A.M. to search ground in vicinity of cross roads on AUTHUILLE-OVILLERS-LA BOISSELLE Road opposite the ?? with a view to ascertaining if the dip in the ground at this point secure from vision and rifle fire could be used by the enemy as an assembling place. Officer i/c Party reported at 4.15 A.M. that at least 100 men could assemble at this spot and gain clear 200 yards advance. Enemy rifle grenades were fired in the afternoon well away to our right. 1 fell about 5 P.M. at Sap head at 140. No damage done.

Supporting Points P.1.   P.2.   6th Seaforth Highrs.

Enemy's Art. did not retaliate on this sector to our Art. bombardment. M.G. fire was opened at intervals on our front trenches during the evening and enemy rifle fire was normal. Our No. 3 Gun fired bursts at the right Sap at Point 424 during the night which had been damaged by our Artillery.
The shelters are not weatherproof. Several in the neighbourhood of Post LONDON have fallen in and these cannot be put into a satisfactory state short of taking them down and rebuilding them. This also applies to Post DORSET. 1 or 2 shelters are at present being re-constructed.

                                                              Brig. Gen.
                                                        Comdg. 152nd Inf. Brigade.

13th November, 1915.

2.

Officer Commanding,
1/5th Seaforth Highrs, 1/6th Argyll & Suth'd Highrs.
1/6th   do.   , 1/8th   do.

Forwarded for your information.

Captain,
Staff Captain,
152nd Infantry Brigade.

13th November 1915.

CONFIDENTIAL
No. 134
152nd INF. BDE.

8N.

51st

WAR DIARY

OF

1/6th. Argyll & Sutherland Highlanders.

From   1st. December, 1915.
To   31st. December, 1915.

....

Vol VIII

CONFIDENTIAL
No. 134 / 52nd INF. BDE.

C O N F I D E N T I A L.

W A R   D I A R Y.

of

1/6th. Battn. Arg. and Suth'd. Highrs.

FROM, 1st. Dec., 1915 TO, 31st. Dec., 1915.

VOLUME X.

Army Form C. 2118.
Volume X.
Page 1.

WAR DIARY
INTELLIGENCE SUMMARY
(Erase heading not required.)

1/6th A.I.S.H. 152nd INF. BDE. No. 13?

Place	Date	Hour	Summary of Events and Information	Remarks and references to Appendices
THIEPVAL.	1/12/15		Battalion in Fire Trenches. Situation generally quiet. Draft of 111 men posted to Coys.	
G.2.	2/12/15		Battalion in Fire Trenches. Nothing to report.	
	3/12/15		Battalion in Fire Trenches	
	4/12/15		Battalion in Fire Trenches. Captain & Adj. A.E. Thomas returned from leave.	
	5/12/15		Battalion in Fire Trenches. Combined shoot by artillery, Stokes mortars with French mortars but did little damage.	
	6/12/15		Battalion in Fire Trenches. Arrangements made for relief. About 2 p.m. battalion was relieved by 5th Seaforths. Coys. relieved independently and proceeded as relieved to AUTHUILLE. (1 pm Battalion in Brigade Reserve at AUTHUILLE.) (Ref ALBERT. 1/40000. Q.3.6c.)	
AUTHUILLE	7/12/15		Battalion in Brigade Reserve. Working parties found for work in Front Line. About 4.10 enemy sent over 10 howitzer shells but without doing any damage.	
"	8/12/15		Battalion in Brigade Reserve. Working parties found for work in Front Line.	
"	9/12/15		Battalion in Brigade Reserve. Working parties found for work in Front Line.	
"	10/12/15		Battalion in Brigade Reserve. Operation orders received, ordering relief	
"	11/12/15		Battalion relieved by 1/7th Royal Highrs. Companies marched off independently as relieved,	
HENENCOURT			taking over Rest Billets at HENENCOURT.	

Army Form C. 2118.

WAR DIARY
or
INTELLIGENCE SUMMARY.

(Erase heading not required.)

1/6th A.Y.S.H

152nd INF. BDE.

Place	Date	Hour	Summary of Events and Information	Remarks and references to Appendices
HENENCOURT.	12/2/15		Battalion in Rest Billets. Cleaning up; kit inspections. Musketry instruction of new draft under Lieut. L.L. Shearer and selected N.C.Os.	
"	13/2/15		Battalion in Rest Billets. Training under 6oy Officers. Recruits' musketry instruction.	
"	14/2/15		Battalion in Rest Billets. Training under 6oy. Officers. Recruits musketry instruction.	
"	15/2/15		Battalion in Rest Billets. 300 men supplied for work in Front Line Defences. Operation order received ordering reliefs.	
"	16/2/15		Battalion relieved 1/4. Royal Lancs. Regt. in sub-sector F.1. Left billets 10·30 a.m.; dinner on the road; relief commenced 2 p.m. Battalion in position 4·30 p.m.	
		8·30 p.m.	Enemy fired 3 rifle grenades, the first of which burst near head of Birmingham Street killing one man, seriously wounding Captain F. McLang and one man. Captain A. CRAIG slightly wounded (at duty). The men killed and wounded belonged to 2/2nd. Highland Field Company. R.E. The trenches in the portion of the line are in very bad condition, having fallen in owing to rain and frost. In some portions of the front line the men are standing knee deep in muddy water. Battalion on Right: 16th. Lancashire Fusiliers Battalion on Left: 6th. Seaforth Highlanders	

Army Form C. 2118.

WAR DIARY
or
INTELLIGENCE SUMMARY

(Erase heading not required.)

1/6th Bn. Arg. & Suth'ds, Highrs
1st 34
152nd INF. BDE.

Page 3

Place	Date	Hour	Summary of Events and Information	Remarks and references to Appendices
Fl. SECTOR - OVILLERS	17-12-15		Battalion in Fire Trenches. Situation quiet on this portion of front. A. & C. Coys. relieved by 2 coys. of 11th. Border Regt. and proceeded to billets in AVELUY.	
"	18-12-15		Battalion in Fire Trenches. Condition of trenches held by B. & D. Coys growing rapidly worse, the men standing thigh deep in water in the fire trench.	
"	19-12-15		Battalion in Fire Trenches. B. & D Coys and Battn. H.Q. relieved by 11th. Border Regt. Relief commenced 2.30 pm. and completed by 5 pm. Battalion billeted in Brigade Reserve at AVELUY	
AVELUY	20-12-15		Battalion in Brigade Reserve. Working parties supplied for work on Fire Trenches.	
"	21-12-15		Battalion in Brigade Reserve. Working parties supplied for work on Fire Trenches.	
"	22-12-15		Battalion in Brigade Reserve. Working parties supplied for work on Fire Trenches.	
"	23-12-15		Battalion in Brigade Reserve. Relieved 5pm. by 16th. H.L.I. Proceeded by platoons at 300 yards distance to billets in Divisional Reserve at MARTINSART	
MARTINSART	24-12-15		Battalion in Divisional Reserve. Cleaning up. Inspection of Battalion in marching order by G.O. Companies, Machine Gun and D stores inspected separately.	
"	25-12-15		Battalion in Divisional Reserve. Working parties furnished. Men not (otherwise) on duty free for sport etc. as far as possible	

WAR DIARY
INTELLIGENCE SUMMARY

Army Form C. 2118.

1/6th A. & S. H.

Pages

Instructions regarding War Diaries and Intelligence Summaries are contained in F. S. Regs., Part II. and the Staff Manual respectively. Title pages will be prepared in manuscript.

No. 134
1/52nd INF. BDE.

Place	Date	Hour	Summary of Events and Information	Remarks and references to Appendices
MARTINSART.	26/12/15		Battalion in Divisional Reserve. Route Marching. Working parties.	
"	27/12/15		Battalion in Divisional Reserve. Route Marching. Working parties. Operation order received ordering move of Battalion to Rear Area. Preparations for move to Rear Area.	
"	28/12/15	9 am	Battalion paraded in marching order with 1st and 2nd Line Transport and extra baggage wagons for move to Rear Area. Route as follows:- MARTINSART- HEDAUVILLE- BEAUCOURT. Battalion billeted in BEAUCOURT for the night.	
BEAUCOURT.	29/12/15	9.30 am	March resumed. Route:- BEAUCOURT- MOLLIENS-AU-BOIS- VILLERS BOCAGE. Battalion arrived in VILLERS BOCAGE about 12.30 pm. Billets allotted proved very unsatisfactory. Arrangements being made to improve accommodation.	
VILLERS BOCAGE.	30/12/15		Battalion in Rest Billets. Programme of training for week ending 1st Jan., 1916 submitted. Cleaning up of clothing and equipment.	
"	31/12/15		Battalion in Rest Billets. Squad drill. Musketry. Subaltern Officers under Regtl. Sergt. Major. Lecture to Officers and Sergeants on "Discipline".	

N.J. Warren
LIEUT. COL.,
CMDG. 6TH A.&G. & SUTHᴅ HIGHʳˢ

Army Form C. 2118.

WAR DIARY
or
INTELLIGENCE SUMMARY.
(Erase heading not required.)

CONFIDENTIAL
Title pages 134
152nd INF. BDE.

Place	Date	Hour	Summary of Events and Information	Remarks and references to Appendices

Casualties for December:—

	Officers	O.R.
K.	1 ×	1
W.	1 ×	4
M.	—	—

× Capt. J. M. Lang.
× Capt. A. Craig; slight; at duty.

Summary of Weekly States for December:—

Week ending.	(1) Fighting Strength last week		(2) Increase for Week		(3) Decrease for Total of (1)+(2)		(4) Decrease for Week		(5) Fighting Strength		(6) Detached from Unit	
	O.	O.R.	O.	O.R.	O.	O.R.	O.	O.R.	O.	O.R.	O.	O.R.
4/12/15	26	652	—	111	26	763	—	9	26	754	8	87
11/12/15	26	754	—	16	26	770	—	22	26	748	9	99
18/12/15	26	748	—	—	26	748	1	13	25	735	9	94
25/12/15	25	735	—	—	25	735	—	10	25	725	9	85
1/1/16	25	725	4	13	29	738	—	20	29	718	11	77

CONFIDENTIAL
No. 134
152nd INF. BDE.

1/6th. BATTN. ARG. & SUTH'D. HIGHRS.

C O N F I D E N T I A L.

W A R D I A R Y.

FOR

JANUARY, 1916.

51st Div.

Vol IX

WAR DIARY
~~INTELLIGENCE SUMMARY~~

Army Form C. 2118.
Volume XI
Page 1

1/6th A.9.S.H.

Place	Date	Hour	Summary of Events and Information	Remarks and references to Appendices
Ref. Map AMIENS Sheet 12 1/80000				
VILLERS BOCAGE	1/1/16		Battalion in Rest Billets. Billet inspection in morning, remainder of day being devoted to sport etc.	
"	2/1/16		Battalion in Rest Billets. Close order drill, musketry etc. Classes in grenade throwing, signalling and machine gun commenced training. (Vide Training Programme)	App. I.
"	3/1/16		Battalion in Rest Billets. Training as for 2nd.	App. 2.
"	4/1/16 10:30am		Battalion moved to new Billeting Area at RUBEMPRE arriving 12 noon.	
RUBEMPRE	5/1/16		Battalion in Rest Billets. Company training, classes etc. as before.	
"	6/1/16		Battalion in Rest Billets. Training as per Training Programme	
"	7/1/16		Battalion in Rest Billets. Training as per Training Programme	
"	8/1/16		Battalion in Rest Billets. Training as per Training Programme	
"	9/1/16		Battalion in Rest Billets. Training as per Training Programme	
"	10/1/16		Battalion in Rest Billets. Training as per Training Programme	
"	11/1/16		Battalion in Rest Billets.	
"	12/1/16		Battalion in Rest Billets. Training as per Training Programme.	
"	13/1/16		Battalion in Rest Billets. Training as per Training Programme.	
"	14/1/16		Battalion in Rest Billets. Training as per Training Programme.	
"	15/1/16		Battalion in Rest Billets. Training as per Training Programme	App. 2.

WAR DIARY

INTELLIGENCE SUMMARY. 1/6th Arg. & Suth. Highrs. Page 2

Army Form C. 2118.

(Erase heading not required.)

Place	Date	Hour	Summary of Events and Information	Remarks and references to Appendices
RUBEMPRE	16-1-16		Battalion in Rest Billets. Divine Service.	
"	17-1-16		Battalion in Rest Billets. Training as per Training Programme.	App. 3.
"	18-1-16		do. do. do.	
"	19-1-16		do. do. do.	
"	20-1-16		Battalion in Rest Billets. Inspection of 1st Line Transport of Brigade by Corps Commander.	
"	21-1-16		Battalion in Rest Billets. Took part in Brigade Tactical Scheme.	
"	22-1-16		Battalion paraded in marching order with 1st Line Transport at 9-30 a.m. and proceeded to ACHEUX in relief of 1/6th Seaforth for work on railway.	App. 3
ACHEUX	23-1-16		Battalion in Billets. No fatigues. Divine Service.	
"	24-1-16		Battalion employed on making new Railway from CANDAS to ACHEUX. Lewis M.G. Section and Signalling Section training as per last week.	
"	25-1-16		do. do. do.	
"	26-1-16		do. do. do.	
"	27-1-16		do. do. do.	
"	28-1-16		do. do. do.	

Army Form C. 2118.

1/6th Battn Arg. & Suth'd High's
Page. 3.

WAR DIARY
INTELLIGENCE SUMMARY.
(Erase heading not required.)

Instructions regarding War Diaries and Intelligence Summaries are contained in F. S. Regs., Part II. and the Staff Manual respectively. Title pages will be prepared in manuscript.

Place	Date	Hour	Summary of Events and Information	Remarks and references to Appendices
ACHEUX	29.1.16		Battalion in ACHEUX. morning taken up with cleaning billets. Battalion paraded in marching order at 1.30 pm. and proceeded to Rest billets at RUBEMPRE.	
"	30.1.16		Battalion in Rest Billets. Divine Service.	
"	31.1.16		Battalion in Rest Billets. Training as per training programme.	M/k. A.

1577 Wt.W10791/1773 500,000 1/15 D. D. & L. A.D.S.S./Forms/C. 2118.

WAR DIARY
INTELLIGENCE SUMMARY.
(Erase heading not required.)

Army Form C. 2118.

1/6th Arg. & Suthd. Highrs.

Page H

Instructions regarding War Diaries and Intelligence Summaries are contained in F. S. Regs., Part II. and the Staff Manual respectively. Title pages will be prepared in manuscript.

Place	Date	Hour	Summary of Events and Information	Remarks and references to Appendices

Casualties during month

	Officers	Other ranks
K.	x	x
W.	x	x
M.	x	x

Date	Fighting strength last week		Increase		Total from (1)+(2)		Decrease		Fighting strength		Not actually with unit	
	O	O.R.	O	O.R.	O	O.R.	O	O.R.	O	O.R.	O	O.R.
8th Jan. 1916.	29.	718.	1	—	30	718	1.	11	29.	707	7.	93.
15th Jan. 1916.	29.	707.	—	9.	29.	716	—	22.	29.	694	7.	105.
22nd Jan. 1916.	29.	694.	—	4	29.	698.	2.	46.	27.	652	7.	107.
29th Jan. 1916.	27.	652	5	10.	32.	662.	—	11	32.	651	7.	125.

B.J. Manson
LIEUT.-COL.
CMDG. 6TH ARG. & SUTHND HIGHRS

APPENDICES. for January. 1916.

2. TRAINING PROGRAMME.

3. TRAINING PROGRAMME.

TRAINING PROGRAMME FOR WEEK ENDING, 8TH. JANUARY, 1916.
1/6th. Batt. Arg. & Suth'd. Highrs.

DAY	9-30 – 12-30	2-30 – 4-30	PLACE	6 p.m.	REMARKS.
MONDAY. 3rd.	Close order drill ½ hour. Bayonet fighting ½ hour. Musketry exercises and extended order drill 2 hrs. One Coy. digging trenches.	Physical training and running.	Ground EAST of Billets.	Lecture on Tactical Scheme.	One Coy. will practice with tube helmets on Mon., Wed., Thur., & Sat. A rifle range is being made for snipers who will practice daily. Grenadier class of 4 N.C.O and 32 O.R. daily-one half during forenoon and remainder in afternoon. Lewis gun teams training daily. Subaltern Officers'class Monday morning, Thursday and Saturday.
TUESDAY. 4th.	Route March via TALMAS-RUBEMPRE-VILLERS BOCAGE Scheme attached.	4p.m. Company lectures. Duties of scouts sentries, guards, care of arms and ammunition.			
WEDNESDAY. 5th.	Close order drill and Running Drill. Practice attack by Coys. against trenches.	HALF HOLIDAY.	Ground EAST of Billets.		
THURSDAY, 6th.	Same as Monday.	Running Drill and Bayonet Fighting.		Same as for Monday.	
FRIDAY. 7th.	Route March via FIESSELLES -POULAINCOURT-VILLERS BOCAGE Scheme attached.			Company lectures in the evening.	
SATURDAY, 8th.	Practice Battalion attack. Musketry and against trenches. Inspection of Billets.	Bayonet Fighting.			

31st. Dec., 1915.

UNIT. 1/6th. Battn. Arg. & Suth'd. Highrs.

DATE.	HOUR OF ASSEMBLY.	PLACE.	DURATION OF TRAINING.	NATURE OF TRAINING TO BE CARRIED OUT.
10th. Jan.	9-30a.m. &o 2-30p.m.	½ mile NORTH of RUBEMPRE.	3hours morning & 3 hours afternoon. morning only. afternoon only. 9-30a.m.-12-30p.m. and 2-30p.m.-4-30p.m.	3 Officers, 1 N.C.O. and 8 men per Platoon at (trench making trenches(¼ in morning and ¼ in afternoon.) 1 Officer and 20 men, Sniping Course. 1 Officer and 1 man per Coy. and Lewis Gun Team, Range Taking Course 16 stretcher bearers under M.O. Signallers according to programme sent in. Lewis Gun Section. In morning with companies. COMPANIES ½ hour, Running and physical training. Musketry and Bayonet fighting. 1 company training with tube helmets and goggles. 1 company digging outlines of trenches. During afternoon,1 company lecture on gas attacks.
11th. Jan.	9-30a.m.	Battn. H.Q.	9-30a.m. -2p.m. Noon. 4p.m.	Route March via PIERREGOT-MOLLIENS AU BOIS-X roads ½ mile NORTH OT ST. GRATIEN- BEAUOURT- RUBEMPRE. SCHEME.:- The Battn. acting as rear guard to a force retiring NORTH through RUBEMPRE will take up a defensive position SOUTH of that village while the force billets for the night. Grenadiers' Course. Range Taking as for Monday 1 company,lecture on gas attacks. Remainder,care of arms etc.
12th. Jan.	10a.m.	Company Parade Grounds.	10a.m. -11-30a.m. 11-45-12-30p.m.	Marching Order Inspection. Running and Physical Training. 1 company practise with tube helmets. Grenadiers as for Monday. Range taking as for Monday.
13th. Jan.	9-30a.m. and 2-30p.m.	Batth. Parade Ground NORTH of RUBEMPRE	9-30-12-30p.m. 2-30 -4-30p.m. 6p.m.	As for Monday. do do Lecture to Officers and N.C.O,s " Organisation of the Army" (By Capt. L-Coats.)
14th. Jan.	9-30a.m.	Battn. H.Q.	9-30a.m.	ROUTE MARCH:- VIA VILLERS BOCAGE-RAINVILLE- PIERREGOT-RUBEMPRE. The Batth. will form part of a force attacking an enemy in position on the line VILLERS BOCAGE- PIERREGOT-MIRVAUX, the frontage allotted to the Unit being just WEST of the RAINVILLE- PIERREGOT Road.
15th. Jan.				

DATE	HOUR OF ASSEMBLY	PLACE.	DURATION OF TRAINING	NATURE OF TRAINING TO BE CARRIED OUT.
15th. Jan.	9-30a.m. 2-30p.m.	Battalion Parade Ground, North of RUBEMPRE.	9-30-12-30p.m.	As for Monday. Trench attack drill by Companies.

N.Maurer   Lieut.Col.,
Commanding,1/6th.A. & S. H.

8th. January, 1915.

UNIT 1/6th. BN. ARGL & SUTH'D. HIGHRS.

PROGRAMME OF TRAINING FOR WEEK ENDING 22nd. JANUARY, 1916.

DATE.	HOUR OF ASSEMBLY.	PLACE.	DURATION OF TRAINING.	NATURE OF TRAINING TO BE CARRIED OUT.
17/1/16.	9 - 30 a.m.	½ mile North of RUBEMPRE.	9-30 a.m. - 12-30 Noon	4 Officers, 1 N.C.O. and 8 men per Platoon. Battn. Grenade School, ½ in morning & half in afternoon. 1 Officer (On leave) 2 N.C.O's and 2 men Scouting & Sniping Course. 1 Officer, 1 N.C.O or 1 man & Lewis Gun Team, Range Taking Course. 16 Stretcher Bearers under Medical Officer. Signallers according to Programme sent in. Lewis Gun Section. Afternoons only until Guns Received Mornings with Coys. As soon as Guns received the reserve section will also begin training. COMPANIES. Remainder of 1 Company on fatigues, bed - making and preparing horse standings. 1 Company:- Tube Helmets & Goggles. Coy. in attack. 1 Company "Trench attack" 1 Company:- Coy. Drill, Musketry etc.
	2 - 30 p.m.	"	2-30 p.m. - 4-30 p.m.	1 Company on fatigue. 1 Company Running etc. & Gas Lecture. 2 Coys. Running, physical drill, Bayonet Fighting & Musketry. Lecture on "Duties" by Adjutant.
	5 - 30 p.m.	Girls School.		
18/1/16.	9 a.m.	Battn. H.Q.	9 a.m. to 1-30 p.m.	ROUTE MARCH H.Q. & Advance Guard Action via PIERREGOT - MOLLIENS - AU - BOIS - CROSS ROADS ½ mile NORTH of ST. GRATIEN. Here the column will come under Artillery fire from direction of CARDONNETTE. Battn. scouts will proceed direct from RUBEMPRE to RAINVILLE & will work eastward with flags to represent 2 Coys. & 1 Machine Gun Firing, the Battn to deploy & attack the ridge EAST of the line RAINVILLE - CARDONNETTE. Return March via RAINVILLE - PIERRGOT. Specialists training as for Monday.

PAGE 2.

UNIT. 1/6th. BATTN. ARG. & SUTH'D. HIGHRS.

CONTD. PROGRAMME OF TRAINING FOR WEEK ENDING 22nd. JANUARY, 1916.

DATE.	HOUR OF ASSEMBLY.	PLACE.	DURATION OF TRAINING.	NATURE OF TRAINING TO BE CARRIED OUT.
18/1/16.	3 - 30 p.m. 5 - 30 p.m.	BILLETS. Girls School.	3-30 p.m. to 4-30 p.m.	Company Lectures. Lecture for Officers and N.C.O's "Esprit de Corps" and Customs of the Service" by Lieut. J. S. Paton (Last from Army School of Instruction).
19/1/16. half holiday	9 - 30 a.m.	½ mile North of RUBEMPRE.	9-30a.m. to 12-30 noon.	As for Monday, but 2 Coys. practice "Trench Attack" as 1st. & 2nd. lines (1 with tube helmets) No fatigues every man on parade.
20/1/16.	9 - 30 a.m.	½ mile North of RUBEMPRE.	9-30 - 12-30 noon 2-30 - 4-30 p.m.	As for Monday. 2 Coys. in morning for "Trench Attack"
21/1/16.	5 - 30 p.m. 9 a.m.	Girls School. Battn. H. Q.	9 a.m. to 2 p.m.	Lecture by Adjutant "Interior Economy". ROUTE MARCH. via VILLERS BOCAGE to carry out "Trench Attack" (Battalion) on trenches South of that place, if arrangements can be made and permission (for use of trenches) granted. No fatigues.
			3-30 to 4-30 p.m. 6 p.m.	Company Lectures. Lecture to Officers. Lessons from "Trench Attack" by Commanding Officer.
22/1/16.	9 a.m.		9 - 30 to 12 noon.	Running Physical Drill & Training, Musketry etc Specialists as for Monday.

All available Subaltern Officers parade on afternoon parades for instruction under a selected Officer
A class of 4 N.C.O's per Company at the same time
under Regtl/Sergt. Major.

15th. January, 1916.

M. Mauren Lieut. Col.
Commanding 1/6th. Bn. A. & S. H.

BATTALION
COPY

Training Programme for Signallers from 10th Jany. till 15th Jany 1916.

6TH A AND S.H

DAY	9AM-10:15AM	10:15AM-11AM	11:30AM-12:30PM	2PM-3PM	3PM-4PM	5:15PM-7:30PM
MONDAY	Buzzer Reading	Flag Reading Station Work	Flag Reading Station Work	Buzzer Reading	Lecture on Company Signalling	Lamp Practice Lamps (Stations) 5pm-7pm
TUESDAY	Do	Lecture on Map Reading	Flag Reading	Do	—	—
WEDNESDAY	Do	Revision in Map Reading	Buzzer Reading	—	—	—
THURSDAY	Do	Test on Map Reading	Flag Reading	Buzzer Reading	—	Lamps (Stations) 5pm-7pm
FRIDAY	Do	Flag Reading	Buzzer Reading	Do	—	Lamp Practice
SATURDAY	Do	BUZZER TEST	FLAG TEST	Do	Do	—

Signallers will take part in all Battalion Tactical Schemes.

9-1-16.

W Macrae, Sig Sgt
Lt A = S/HQ

Instrs - Machine Gun Section. 1/6th A&S Hrs.

Programme of training for week ending 8th Jany. 1916.

	9.30 AM to 12.30 P.M.	2.30 P.M. to 4.30 P.M.
WEDNESDAY.	9.30AM to 10AM. Cleaning & inspection of guns. 10 AM to 11 AM. Lecture. Capt Hardy. 11 AM to 12.30pm. Close order drill & musketry.	HALF HOLIDAY.
THURSDAY.	Class. General description. 2 hours Close order drill & musketry 1 "	Lecture for NCO's 'Discipline' at 4.30pm. Class. 'Mechanism'.
FRIDAY.	Cleaning of guns ½ hr. ROUTE MARCH. 2½ hours.	Class. Mechanism 1 hour Stripping 1 "
SATURDAY.	Stripping 1 hour Close order Musketry 1 hour Mechanism 1 hour	Care and cleaning of gun 1 hour Mechanism 1 hour. Shanks Lt D.C.M.G.

BATTALION COPY

Training Programme for Signallers from 17th Feb. 23rd Jan: 1916

6th A and S.H.

DAY	9–10.15 AM	10.15–11 AM	11.30–12.30	2–3 PM	3–4 PM	5.15–5.30 PM
MONDAY	Buzzer Reading	Cleaning Instruments	Flag Reading	Buzzer Reading	Lecture on Compass Bearings	Lamp Practice
TUESDAY	Do	Lecture on Map Reading	Buzzer Reading	Do	—	Lamp Practice 6.15 PM – 7 PM
WEDNESDAY	Do	Visual Signalling 10.15 AM – 12.30 PM		—	—	—
THURSDAY	Do	Lecture on Previous days work	Flag Reading	Buzzer Reading	—	Lamp Practice 5.15 PM – 7 PM
FRIDAY	Do	Visual Signalling 10.15 AM – 12.30 PM		Do	Buzzer Signalling	Lamp Practice
SATURDAY	Do	BUZZER TEST	FLAG READING TEST	—	—	—

Signallers will take part in all Tactical Schemes of the Battalion

10 Macrae, Sig. Sgt
6th A.S.H.

14/1/16

CONFIDENTIAL
No. 134
152nd INF. BDE.

10 N.

WAR DIARY

OF

1/6th Bn. Argyll & Sutherland Highlanders.

FEBRUARY, 1916.

Vol X

1/6th Avg & Such'd Army Form C. 2118.

Page 1.

WAR DIARY
or
INTELLIGENCE SUMMARY.
(Erase heading not required.)

Place	Date	Hour	Summary of Events and Information	Remarks and references to Appendices
RUBEMPRE.	1.2.16		Battalion in rest billets. Training as per Training Programme.	A/1.
"	2.2.16		Battalion in rest billets. " " " "	"
"	3.2.16		Battalion in rest billets. " " " "	"
"	4.2.16		Battalion in rest billets. 2 Coys. paraded at 1 p.m. and marched to MIRVAUX to rest billets. 6 & A. Coys. paraded at 3 p.m. and marched to rest billets at MOLLIENS AU BOIS.	
MOLLIENS AU BOIS	5.2.16		Battalion in rest billets. Employed in filling in training trenches at RUBEMPRE. Lewis Gun Section, Grenadiers and Signallers training as per programme.	A/1.
"	6.2.16		Battalion in rest billets. Divine Service.	
"	7.2.16		Battalion in rest billets. Training as usual. Lewis Gun Section, Signallers & Grenadiers training as on 5th inst.	
"	8.2.16		Battalion paraded in Marching Order at 9.30 a.m. Guides 1st & 2nd line Transport and extra baggage waggons for move to CORBIE. Route as follows.- via St. Gratin, Querrieux, CORBIE.	
"	9.2.16		Battalion in rest billets. 2 Coys. employed unloading Ammunition	

WAR DIARY
or
INTELLIGENCE SUMMARY.
(Erase heading not required.)

Army Form C. 2118.

1/6th Bn Argyll & Suth'd Highrs

Page 2.

Place	Date	Hour	Summary of Events and Information	Remarks and references to Appendices
CORBIE	9.2.16		At Railway Station, other 2 Coy. training as per usual. Specialist training as usual.	
"	10.2.16		Battalion in rest billets. Training under Coy. arrangements. Specialist training as usual.	
"	11.2.16		Battalion in rest billets. Coy. paraded at 9.30 am for Coy. route march not less than 8 miles. Coy. Commanders to select their own routes. Signallers & Lewis Gun training as usual.	
"	12.2.16		Battalion in rest billets. Training under Coy. arrangements. Afternoon observed as a holiday.	
"	13.2.16		Battalion in rest billets. Divine Service.	
"	14.2.16		Battalion in rest billets. ~~Battalion paraded at 9.30~~ Coy. paraded for inspection by Comdg. Officer. Training as per Training Programme	App. 2.
"	15.2.16		Battalion in rest billets. Battalion paraded in Marching Order with 1st line transport for route march. Wide training Programme.	App. 2.
"	16.2.16		Battalion in rest billets. 2 Coys engaged digging trenches, other 2 Coy. training as per training programme. Afternoon observed as a holiday.	App. 2.
"	17.2.16		Battalion in rest billets. 2 Coys. engaged digging trenches, then 2 Coy. training as per training Programme	App. 2.

WAR DIARY
INTELLIGENCE SUMMARY. 1/6th Bn Argyll & Suth'd High'rs
Page 3

Army Form C. 2118.

Place	Date	Hour	Summary of Events and Information	Remarks and references to Appendices
CORRIE	18.2.16		Battalion in rest billets. All Coys. and details engaged bathing between the hours of 8 am and 3 pm. Training as per training programme.	R/k. 2.
"	19.2.16		Battn. in rest billets. All rifles in Battn. inspected during forenoon. Also lectures on "care of the rifle" were given by Staff-Sergt Franklin of Bde Hqrs. Afternoon therefore as a holiday.	
"	20.2.16		Battn. in rest billets. Divine Service.	
"	21.2.16		Battn. less details paraded at 10 am. under the command of Major R Stewart and marched to DAOURS for work on Railway Bridge — O.C. 110th Railway Coy, VECQUEMONT. Signallers, <s>Snipers</s> and Lewis Gun Sections training as usual. New class of Grenadiers under Battn. Grenadier Officer.	
"	22.2.16		Battn. less Specialists engaged on work at railway at VECQUEMONT. Signallers, Lewis Gun Sections, and new Grenadier Class training as usual.	
"	23.2.16		Battalion less specialists engaged on work on railway at VECQUEMONT. Signallers, Lewis Gun Section, and new Grenadier Class, as usual.	
"	24.2.16		Battn. less specialists engaged on work on railway at VECQUEMONT. Signallers, Lewis Gun Section and new Grenadier Class as usual.	

Army Form C. 2118.

WAR DIARY
or
INTELLIGENCE SUMMARY.

1/6th Aug* Suth* High*
Page 4.

(Erase heading not required.)

Instructions regarding War Diaries and Intelligence Summaries are contained in F. S. Regs., Part II. and the Staff Manual respectively. Title pages will be prepared in manuscript.

Place	Date	Hour	Summary of Events and Information	Remarks and references to Appendices
CORBIE	25-2-16		Battalion engaged in work on railway at VECQUEMONT. Specialists training as for 24th.	
"	26-2-16		do. do.	
"	27-2-16		Battn. engaged on work on railway at VECQUEMONT.	
"	28-2-16		Detachment engaged on work at VECQUEMONT received orders from Division to proceed to CORBIE. Battn. received orders to hold itself in readiness to move on 28th inst.	
"	29-2-16		Battn. moved from CORBIE to PIERROT. Surplus baggage conveyed by motor. Orders received to move to new billeting area of RAINNEVILLE.	

R.Y. Rawson
LIEUT.-COL.
CMDG. 6TH ARG. & SUTHND HIGHRS

1577 Wt. W10791/1773 500,000 1/15 D. D. & L. A.D.S.S./Forms/C. 2118.

BATTALION
BJ637

Signalling Training Programme from 31st Jan. to 5th Feby. 1916

6TH A and S. H.

DAY.	9–10AM	10AM–11AM	11:30AM–12:30PM	2PM–3PM	3PM–4PM	6.15–7PM
MONDAY	Visual Flag Reading	Buzzer Reading	Buzzer Reading	Lamp Reading	Lecture on Compass Reading	Lamp Practice
TUESDAY	BATTA DON	S G M	E M E.	—	—	Lamp Practice
WEDNESDAY	Visual Flag Reading	Buzzer Reading	Buzzer Reading	—	—	—
THURSDAY	BRIG A DE	S H E M E	—	—	Lamp Practice
FRIDAY	Visual Flag Reading	Buzzer Reading	Buzzer Reading	Lamp Reading	Lecture on Map Reading	Lamp Practice
SATURDAY.	FLAG TEST	BUZZER TEST	LAMP TEST	—	—	—

30/1/16

W Macrae, Sig Sgt
6th A and S. H.

SCHEME FOR 1st. FEB.

GENERAL IDEA.   The Germans having broken our Line, have advanced and established themselves on the Line BEAUQUESNES - PUCHEVILLERS - HERRISSART.

The 51st. Division concentrated at FLESSELLES with A.G. of 152nd. Bde. at TALMAS.

SPECIAL IDEA.   152nd. Bde. receives orders to advance on a front of 1500 yards on both sides of TALMAS, - PUCHEVILLERS Road and establish itself as close to the enemy's position as possible.

6th. A. & S. H. having arrived at VAL DE MAISON in Aritllery formation with PUCHEVILLERS as its objective and a Battn. on either flank, finds the enemy entrenched west of PUCHEVILLERS and is ordered to attack on a frontage of 500 yards on both sides of the road and to consolidate a line as near as possible to the German line. Actual defensive position to be taken up by troops which would occupy it.

1/6th. A. & S. H.

Programme of Training for week endg. 5th. Feb.

Date	Hour of Assembly.	Place.	Duration of Training.	Nature of Training to be carried out.
31st.	9-30 a.m.	ground ½ mile N.& NE of RUBEMPRE.	9-30 a.m. to 12-30 & 2-30 to 4-30.	Battn. Grenade School. 4 Officers from Battn.1 N.C.O. & 8 men per platoon to continue Course already begun. Snipers. 1 Officer, 2 N.C.O's & 24 men (6 per Coy) Scout & Sniping Course. Lewis Gun Team & Reserve Team & 3 Officers training under M.G.O. Stretcher Bearers, stretcher drill & work Engineers.
			9-30 a.m. to 12-30 & 2-30 to 4-30.	Signallers, according to Programme sent in. Companies, Musketry, Visual Training, Running and Physical drill. 1 Coy. for Lecture daily during afternoon by M.O. 1 Coy. to attend at Grenade School during morning to learn how to bomb up a communication trench. 1 Coy. ditto in afternoon. All 2nd. Lieuts available under Regtl. Sergt. Major in morning for Communicating drill and Musketry together with Class of 16 N.C.O's. In afternoon, 2nd. Lieuts.under Capt. Robertson for instruction in trench duties, platoon leading etc. Lecture on 1st. Aid etc. by M.O. to Officers & N.C.O's.
	5-30 p.m.	Girls School.	5-30 to 6-30.	
1st. Feb.	9-30 a.m.	Country N of RUBEMPRE.	9-30 to 2 p.m. 5-30 to 6-30.	Scheme attached. No fatigues. All specialists except Bombers on parade. Company lectures. Officers Class as for Monday. N.C.O's Class. Map reading under Sergt. Major.

2nd. Feb. (Wed)	9-30 a.m.	ground ½ mile N & NE of Rubempre.	9-30 a.m. to 12-30 p.m.	As for Monday. Two Coys practice Trench Attack as 1st. and 2nd. Lines, one with Tube Helmets, and receive instruction in the working of grenade parties from Battn. Grenadier Officer.
3rd. Feb.	5-30.	Brigade Day. Girls School	5-30 to 6-30 p.m.	No fatigues. Every man on parade. Lecture on duties and Interior Economy by Adjt. for Officers and N.C.O's.
4th. Feb.	9-30 a.m.	Battn. Training ground.	9-30 to 12-30. 2-30 to 4-30.	As for Monday. 2 Coys for Trench Attack as on Wednesday. N.C.O's. Map reading in afternoon and military vocabulary. Officers class instructed in "Use of Tube Helmets" & Gas Attacks.
5th. Feb.	9-30 a.m.	Company Parades.	9-30 to 10-30. 11 to 12-30. 11 a.m.	Marching Order Parade except Bombers. Battn. Drill under Adjt. Inspection of Transport by C.O.

Fatigues as detailed from one Coy. as far as possible daily.
Baths for 1 Coy. daily on Monday, Tuesday, Wednesday, & Friday.

Lieut. Col.
Comdg. 1/6th. A. & S. H.

APPENDIX 2.

PROGRAMME OF TRAINING FOR WEEK ENDING SATURDAY, 19TH. FEB.

Unit. 1/6th Bn. Arg. & Suthd. Highlanders.

DATE	HOUR OF ASSEMBLY	PLACE.	DURATION OF TRAINING.	NATURE OF TRAINING TO BE CARRIED OUT.
14th. Feb.	11-30 a.m.	Coy. Alarm Posts.	9-30 - 11-30 a.m. 11-30 - 12-30 2-30 - 4-30 p.m. 6 - 7 p.m.	Cleaning and preparation. Marching Order Inspection by C.O. Coy. Training. Officers & N.C.Os Class. Lecture by Maj. Haldane on Artillery.
15th. Feb.	9-30 a.m.	Battn. Alarm Post.	9-30 a.m. 5-30 p.m.	Route March. CORBIE - LA NEUVILLE - LA HOUSSOYE - PONT NOYELLES - LA NEUVILLE - CORBIE. Advanced Guards. Lecture to Officers and N.C.Os. "Surprise and Necessity for readiness" by C.O.
16th. Feb.	9-30 a.m.	Battn. Alarm Posts.	9-30 - 12-30.	Company Training. Officers' Class under Regtl. Sergt. Major. If trenches ready, selected Grenadier Course of 1 N.C.O. and 2 men per platoon to teach how to instruct.
17th. Feb.	9-30 a.m.	Battn. Alarm Posts.	9-30 a.m. 5-30 p.m.	Brigade Training or Battn. inAttack on Bridge over river ANCRE at BONNAY. Scheme attached. Lecture on "My experiences at LOOS" Maj. Gr. Jur.

1/6th BATTALION
ARGYLL & SUTHERLAND HIGHLANDERS
12 FEB 1916

DATE.	HOUR OF ASSEMBLY.	PLACE.	DURATION OF TRAINING.	NATURE OF TRAINING TO BE CARRIED OUT.
18th.Feb.	9-30 a.m.	Battn. Alarm Posts.	9-30-12-30. 2-30 - 4-30.	Coy. Training. Battn. Grenade School as for 16th. Officers Class as usual.
19th.Feb.	10a.m.	Coy.Parades.	10 - 11a.m. 11 - 12-30.	Inspection of Billets by C.O. Care of arms, equipment, and clothing.

Lieut. Col.,

Comdg. 1/6th. A. & S. H.

SCHEME FOR 17TH. FEB.

General Idea.

News having been received that the Germans having taken ALBERT are advancing on AMIENS the Brigade is ordered to take up a position from the RIVER ANCRE at BONNAY Northwards and try and keep the bridge at BONNAY intact. The Bridge North of VAUX is held by the French.

Special Idea.

The 1/6th. A. & S. H. receive orders at 9 a.m. on 17th. February, to march to BONNAY by the direct route from CORBIE and hold the Village and Bridge.

Its scouts report German Mounted scouts in BONNAY.

One Coy. will march earlier by the route North of the ANCRE and act as the enemy.

12th. February, 1916.

M/Mavor Lieut. Col.,
Comdg. 1/6th. A. & S. H.

CONFIDENTIAL
No. 134
152nd INF. BDE.

WAR DIARY.

of

1/6th Bn. Argyll & Sutherland Highlanders.

From

1st March, 1916.

To

31st March, 1916.

WAR DIARY or INTELLIGENCE SUMMARY

Army Form C. 2118.
CONFIDENTIAL No. 134
1/2nd INF. BDE. 1/6th Bn. A. & S. Highrs.
Volume XIII. Page. 1.

Place	Date	Hour	Summary of Events and Information	Remarks and references to Appendices
PIERREGOT.	1/3/16	12 noon	Battalion moved to new Billeting Area at RAINNEVILLE.	
RAINNEVILLE	2/3/16		Companies at disposal of Company Commanders for training.	
"	3/3/16		Company and specialist training in neighbourhood of Billets.	
"	4/3/16		Company and specialist training in neighbourhood of Billets. Operation order received for move to BEAUVAL.	
"	5/3/16	9:30 am	Battalion proceeded by march route as part of Brigade to BEAUVAL, via PIERREGOT - RUBEMPRE - PUCHEVILLERS - BEAUQUESNE - BEAUVAL, arriving 2:30 p.m. 13 Brigade billeted in BEAUVAL during the night. 3 officers visited trenches in new area.	
BEAUVAL.	6/3/16		Battalion billeted in BEAUVAL. Companies and specialists at disposal of Officer Commanding. Feet &c. inspections.	
"	7/3/16		Battalion billeted in BEAUVAL. Companies at disposal of Company Commanders. Gas Lectures by Platoon Commanders.	
"	8/3/16		Battalion billeted in BEAUVAL. Operation order received for move to BEAUDRICOURT.	
"	9/3/16		Battalion proceeded by march route as part of Brigade to BEAUDRICOURT, via DOULLENS - BOUQUEMAISON - LE SOUICH - IVERGNY - BEAUDRICOURT.	
BEAUDRICOURT	10/3/16		Battalion proceeded by march route as part of Brigade to MAREUIL, via AVESNES-LE-COMTE - HABARCQ - MAROEUIL. Distance 13 mls. Bn. completed in excellent marching. By B.O.G.	

Army Form C. 2118.

WAR DIARY
~~INTELLIGENCE SUMMARY~~
(Erase heading not required.)

CONFIDENTIAL
No. 134
152nd INF. BDE.
16th. Bn. A.T. & Highrs.
Page 2

Place	Date	Hour	Summary of Events and Information	Remarks and references to Appendices
MAROEUIL	11/3/16		Battalion in Brigade Reserve. 350 men found for S.A.A. fatigue in Fire Trenches.	
"	12/3/16		Battalion in Brigade Reserve. 350 men found for Guards, Working Parties etc.	
"	13/3/16		Battalion in Brigade Reserve. 350 men found for Guards, Working Parties, etc.	
"	14/3/16		Battalion in Brigade Reserve. Reinforcement, 52 other ranks arrived from Base.	
"	15/3/16		Battalion in Brigade Reserve. 350 men found for Guards, Working Parties etc.	
"	16/3/16		Battalion in Brigade Reserve. 350 men found for Guards, Working Parties etc.	
"	17/3/16		Battalion in Brigade Reserve. 350 men found for Guards, Working Parties etc.	
"	18/3/16		Battalion in Brigade Reserve. Operation order received ordering relief.	
"	19/3/16		Battalion proceeded to Fire Trenches in LABYRINTH SECTOR, taking over from 8th A.V.S.H. as left Battalion in Brigade Line. Strength:- Fire Trenches 343, Support 147. Relief completed without incident. Unit on Right:- 6th. Seaforth Highrs. Unit on Left:- 5th Gordon Highrs. Weather dry and mild; clear moonlight during night. Trenches in this portion of the line are very close together and there is little rifle fire the chief weapons being hand grenades and mortar bombs. Coys. disposed from right to left as follows:- D, B, A. In support, C.	

WAR DIARY
or
~~INTELLIGENCE~~ SUMMARY.
(Erase heading not required.)

Army Form C. 2118.
CONFIDENTIAL
No. 134

152 INF. BDE.
1/6 B.A. & S. Highrs

Page 3

Place	Date	Hour	Summary of Events and Information	Remarks and references to Appendices
LABYRINTH SECTOR	20.3.16		Hostile Trench Mortars and Snipers active during the night, continuous attempts being made to send T.M. Bombs into Saps D.3 and 5/4. German working party dispersed opposite saps 7.5.4 and 7.6.3 with Lewis Gun and rifle fire. Casualties. Wounded, 2. Enemy inactive during the day except for sniping and grenade throwing. Casualties, nil.	initialled
"	21.3.16			initialled
"	22.3.16	3.30pm	Two 2" T.M. Guns and Stokes guns fired 66 rounds doing considerable damage to enemy trenches. German sniper who was very active at Sap 7.5.4 was silenced by 5 grenades about 8pm. Working party dispersed at 11.15pm. Casualties: Wounded, 3.	initialled
"	23.3.16		Enemy quiet during night. Little sniping. Two Germans observed opposite Sap 7.6.5 wearing hiked helmets with khaki covers. Wind. S.E. Casualties. 2/Lieut A.B. WISHART. 1 man killed, 7 wounded. For account of enemy grenade attack see Appendix. 1.	App.1
"	24.3.16		Grenade fighting from saps continued. Enemy trench mortar blew in sap in C. Coys sub-sector killing Sergeant W. Boyd and wounding 2/Lieut. R.J. SHANKS. Enemy sniper active during the night being replied to by our own. Snow on ground made observation difficult.	initialled

Army Form C. 2118.

WAR DIARY
or
~~INTELLIGENCE SUMMARY.~~
(Erase heading not required.)

CONFIDENTIAL
No. 134

16th. Arg. & Suthd. Highrs 1/52nd INF. BDE.   Page 4.

Place	Date	Hour	Summary of Events and Information	Remarks and references to Appendices
LABYRINTH SECTOR (M.2)	25-3-16		No unusual enemy activity during day. Grenade fighting from Saps and sniping as opportunity offered, which was seldom.	
	26-3-16	2:20am.	Enemy exploded a large mine opposite left company (A. Coy). For full account see Appendix II. Casualties:- Killed 2/Lieut. A. McNeil and 5 other ranks, Wounded 6, Missing 15. The missing men were probably all buried in the craters caused by the explosion; the body of one man was afterwards found by 5th. Gordons on our left.	App. II
	27-3-16		Period of inactivity following events of yesterday morning. Germans seldom expose themselves in M.2. though our trained snipers are on the alert night and day. The enemy appear to rely on their light and heavy Trench Mortars for the destruction of men and trenches and these are very effective. The offensive with this weapon always appeared to be with the enemy. Retaliation requires to be doubled to have the desired effect. Casualties: Killed 3, Wounded 5, Shock 1.	
	28-3-16		Quiet day. Grenade and Trench Mortar fighting. Casualties, Killed, 1. Wounded 1.	
	29-3-16		During the afternoon, enemy fired several light mortars and shelled trenches with shrapnel. Snipers had to vacate posts on right of M.2 on account of enemy's light mortars which were fired for about 2 hours.	

WAR DIARY CONFIDENTIAL
or
INTELLIGENCE SUMMARY No. 134
/52nd INF. BDE. 1/6th A.Y.& Highrs.

Army Form C. 2118.
Page 5.

Place	Date	Hour	Summary of Events and Information	Remarks and references to Appendices
SUB-SECTOR M.2.	30.3.16		Time quiet except for occasional grenades and trench mortar bombs. Orders issued for relief of Battn. by 8th. Argylls on 31st. inst.	
(LABYRINTH)	31.3.16	3.40am	Two more mines in the space of 5 days were exploded by the enemy within a few yards of our front trenches near Sap 762. Immediately after the explosion the Germans (overwhelmed prisoner left in early) attacked our sap heads but were repulsed with heavy loss. Immediately after the explosion the a heavy barrage by enemy artillery, trench mortars, machine guns etc. was formed on our support trenches. All raids again behaved splendidly. our losses being 2 Officers wounded (2/Lieut. W. FORSYTH - seriously, 2/Lieut. W.S. MUIR - at duty) 2 Sgts. 1 Cpl. and 3 Ptes. killed; 14 other ranks wounded. Total Casualties for March, 1916 :- Killed. 1 Officer 19 O.R. Wounded. 4 " 48 " } Total 5 Officer 82 " O.R. Missing — 14 " Shock. 3	

Fighting Strength 31st March, 30 Officers, 561 Other Ranks.

M.M. .... LIEUT.-COL.
C. in EG. 6TH ARG. & SUTHND HIGHRS

Appendix 1

CONFIDENTIAL
No. 134

Head Quarters,
51st (Highland) Division.

DAILY INTELLIGENCE SUMMARY.

5th Seaforth Highrs. (Right Sub-Sector).

During the forenoon enemy shelled our left front lines without causing any damage. After dusk and up to mid-night enemy were active with Rifle Grenades and light T.M.Bombs. We replied with T.M. Bombs. Things were quiet till about 6.A.M. when 2 large T.M.Bombs fell harmlessly into our lines.

A party went out from Sap 126 and lay out in the hope of cutting off any party of the enemy who might come out, but none appeared. Movement was audible and a sniper fired from Sap opposite to where this party was, and grenades were thrown into the Sap. Ten minutes after, the enemy responded with grenades but our party had returned. We think the enemy suffered some casualties.

Opposite M enemy have a device for throwing hand grenades. Opposite S a German working party was seen and dispersed by rifle fire. The enemy appear very active in trench at square B.13. and B.19.

Several small enemy periscopes were smashed during the day.
Wind N.N.E.

6th Argyll & Suth'd Highrs (Left Sub-Sector).

At 1.P.M. enemy made a grenade attack from crater on point 765. which lasted till 2.15.P.M. Enemy were very close and forced us to retire down Sap. 2nd Lieut A.LANG., and Corpl: QUINN, and Pte:BARBER, forced Germans back and continued throwing grenades until reinforced by Battalion Grenadiers under 2nd Lieut: A.B.WISHART, who poured grenades into the enemy and must have caused many casualties. This action by the Battalion Grenadiers was supported by our Stokes and 2" T.M.'s and 1 Lewis Gun, which was fired from the parapet by 2nd Lieut:J.H.COATS. Enemy grenades were completely silenced by 2.P.M. During the action 2nd Lieut:WISHART, was wounded and one man killed and 4 wounded. The enemy kept up T.M. bombardment on 765. and 767. till about 3.P.M. our T.M's replying. The parapet at 765. was blown in crushing one man who was dug out. All damage was repaired during the night. Our grenadiers threw over 1,000 French Grenades and completely silenced enemy. Many German grenades failed to explode. We threw 200 grenades into German Sap opposite 277, the German reply being weak. At 5.P.M. the enemy fired 3 T.M's and grenades into 767 and 766. We replied with Stokes Gun and grenades, one man being severely wounded.

                            (Sgd). T.M.Booth,
                            for Brigadier General,
24th March 1916.   Commanding 152nd Infantry Brigade.

                     (2).

Officer Commanding,
   1/5th Seaforth Highrs , 1/6th Argyll & Suth'd Highrs.
   1/6th   do.   , 1/8th   do.
   152nd Infantry Brigade Machine Gun Company.
   51/X. Trench Mortar Battery.
   152/1.   do.
   152/2.   do.

         For your information, please.

                                      Captain,
                                      Staff Captain,
24th March 1916.   152nd Infantry Brigade.

Head Quarters.

51st (Highland) Division.

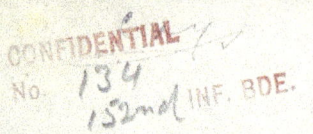

Appendix 2

DAILY INTELLIGENCE SUMMARY.

M.1. 6th Seaforth Highrs.

We relieved the 5th Seaforth Highrs in M.1. at 4.P.M. The night was very quiet on this point except for slight bombing activity from our left Company Saps. The enemy fired 2 Trench Mortar Bombs on our left Company's front, neither of which exploded.

About 2.20 A.M. a mine was heard to explode on our left in M.2. followed by the sound of bursting grenades. At 8.15.A.M. one of our 6" guns fired several rounds on enemy positions on ridge south of VIMY., Wind Strong S.S.E.

M.2. 6th Argyll & Suth'd Highrs.

As previously reported the enemy exploded a large mine at Point 766, followed by a heavy bombardment on our front trench with Shrapnel and Trench Mortars. Many men were buried as a result of the explosion and 5 were killed outright (including 2/Lt.McNEIL). 2nd Lieut:McNEIL was shot by a sniper while going up to render assistance at Point 767,. So far as can be ascertained 15 14 are missing and it is presumed their bodies lie buried in the crater. In addition 3 other men are wounded and a few more suffering from shock. Shell fire may have accounted for some of those who were killed at the time of the explosion. Prior to the explosion a patrol from the 6th Argyll & Sutherland Highrs consisting of 2nd Lieut:FORSYTH, an N.C.O. and 8 men went out from Point 768, with the object of capturing the occupants of a German Shelter the exact locality of which had been established by a patrol from the same Battalion on the 24th March. The patrol encountered a German patrol numbering 15 men led by two men who retired on observing our patrol. The two Gremans went back to a ridge where our patril clearly observed the grey-blue uniform of the remainder of the enemy patrol, by the flare of a Very light. The Germans were evidently lying in wait for our patrol who withdrew after being out for one hour and twenty minutes. As already reported in my morning wire, Artillery support was asked for at 2.22.A.M. but no gun fired till 2.45.A.M. - 23 minutes.

Brigade Machine Gun Company.

Indirect fire scheme was carried out on trenches 17.D.4.2. and between 11.D.7.1. and 12.C.4.4. 750 rounds fired in each case. A noise like a steam engine was heard at 15.A.11. about 11.P.M.

(Sgd).T.M.Booth, Major,
for Brigadier General,
Commanding 152nd Infantry Brigade.

26th March 1916.

For information, please.

Captain,
Staff Captain,
152nd Infantry Brigade.

26th March 1916.

WAR DIARY

of

1/6th Bn. Arg. & Suth'd. Highlanders.

From

1st April, 1916.

To

30th April, 1916.

Confidential.

War Diary

of

1/6th. Battn. Arg. and Suthd. Highrs.

From. 1/4/16 To. 30/4/16

WAR DIARY or INTELLIGENCE SUMMARY

1/6th A.S.&.H.

Army Form C. 2118.
Volume XIV
Page 1.

Place	Date	Hour	Summary of Events and Information	Remarks and references to Appendices
LABYRINTH SECTOR	1/4/16		Battalion in Brigade Reserve in subsector M. Two companies supporting 8th. Argylls one company at Adv. Bde. H.Q., one company at MAROEUIL.	
"	2/4/16		Battalion in Brigade Reserve. Working parties and water carrying parties found for Fire Trenches.	
"	3/4/16		Battalion in Brigade Reserve. Working parties etc. found for Fire Trenches.	
"	4/4/16		Battalion in Brigade Reserve. Working parties etc. found. Letter received from S.S. Assn. intimating that a bequest of £100, less legacy duty, had been left by Mrs. Jane Hamilton, 38, Millbrae Crescent, Langside for behoof of disabled soldiers belonging to Renfrew.	App. I.
"	5/4/16		Battalion in Brigade Reserve. Operation order ordering relief.	
"	6/4/16		Battalion relieved 8th. Argylls (less one company) in Fire Trenches in sub-sector No. 2. Reliefs completed by 12 noon. Companies distributed as follows. Front Trench D Coy. 2 Platoons C. Coy. A. Coy. 8th. Argylls. Support Trench B Coy. 2 Platoons C. Coy. Local Reserve A. Coy. Total Strength in Trenches 435 rifles. Battalion on right 6th. Seaforths. Battalion on left 7th. Gordons.	
"	7/4/16		Battalion in Fire Trenches. Quiet night with little activity	
"	8/4/16		Battalion in Fire Trenches. During the day enemy activity confined to sniping	

Army Form C. 2118.

WAR DIARY
or
INTELLIGENCE SUMMARY.
(Erase heading not required.)

1/6th A. & S. H.   Page 2.

Place	Date	Hour	Summary of Events and Information	Remarks and references to Appendices
	8-4-16	6p.m.	Our artillery bombarded enemy trenches immediately in front of our position. All shells burst well and considerable damage appears to have been caused. Enemy retaliated with shrapnel, light and heavy trench mortars. From 8pm. to 8.25pm a Battalion fire scheme was carried out on enemy trenches in co-operation with artillery.	
	9-4-16		Enemy quiet all day, offering few opportunities for sniping. At 3pm enemy fired several shells and trench mortars, our artillery retaliating.	
	10-4-16	3.15am	Enemy exploded a mine under Sap 765 on our right company's front. Enemy did not open fire and near lip of crater was occupied by us. Casualties :- 2 killed 1 wounded, 4 missing believed to be buried. A slow barrage was carried out by our artillery during subsequent rescue operations on account of enemy's sniping activity concentrated on the crater. In the afternoon battalion was relieved by 5th Argylls and proceeded to Post ARIANE as Battalion in Brigade Reserve.	
	11-4-16		Battalion in Brigade Reserve. The following recommendations for Awards in connection with the recent enemy mining operations have been made by the C.O.	

Army Form C. 2118.
Page 3.

WAR DIARY
INTELLIGENCE SUMMARY

(Erase heading not required.)

1/6th A. & S. Highrs.

Place	Date	Hour	Summary of Events and Information	Remarks and references to Appendices
			For Operations on 31st. March, 1916.	
			Captain D. N. Robertson, Military Cross.	
			2/Lieutenant, E. A. McKechnie, Military Cross.	
			2091. Pte. J. Flynn. D.C.M. (Immediate)	
			3019, L.Cpl. A. Wilson, D.C.M. (Immediate)	
			3564. L.Cpl. J. Newnam, Mention in Despatches. (Since killed in action)	
			79. Pte. J. McPhail. D.C.M. (Immediate)	
			1645. Pte. A. Wilson D.C.M. (Immediate.)	
			For Operations on 10th. April, 1916	
			2/Lieutenant, J. M. Caldwell Military Cross.	
			367. Sergeant J. McRae. D.C.M. (Immediate)	
MAROEUIL	12-4-16		Battalion in Brigade Reserve. Operation order ordering relief. Battalion relieved by 6th. Seaforths and proceeded to Billets in Divisional Reserve at MAROEUIL.	
"	13-4-16		Battalion in Divisional Reserve. Bathing of N.C.O.s and men at Divisional Baths. Working parties supplied for R.E. and Town Major.	
"	14-4-16		Battalion in Divisional Reserve. Working parties supplied for R.E. and Town Major.	

WAR DIARY / INTELLIGENCE SUMMARY

Army Form C. 2118

1/6th A. & S. Highrs

Page 4.

Place	Date	Hour	Summary of Events and Information	Remarks and references to Appendices
MARŒUIL	15-4-16		Battalion in Divisional Reserve. Working parties for R.E. and Town Major. Operation Order No. 4 issued, arranging for relief of 1/5th Argylls in M.2 Sector.	App. 2
LABYRINTH SECTOR (M.2)	16-4-16		Battalion relieved 1/8th Argylls in M.2. Sector. All reliefs completed by 6 p.m. Quiet night except for occasional sniping. Our artillery opened a heavy barrage at midnight. Enemy sent up a large number of flares. Owing to clearness of the night and enemy's alertness it was difficult to reconnoitre damage done. Patrol sent out at 2 am reported enemy trench at A.16.C.9/85 to be badly damaged.	
	17-4-16		Battalion in Fire Trenches. Short hostile bombardment during forenoon doing slight damage to communication trenches and support line.	
	18-4-16		Battalion in Fire Trenches. Situation generally quiet with occasional sniping and trench mortar activity.	
	19-4-16		Battalion in Fire Trenches. Official intimation received that the following Honours and Rewards have been granted to Officers and Men of the Battalion by the Field Marshal Commanding-in-Chief:— Date of Award. 18th April, 1916. 1. 3rd. (Special Reserve) Battn. Princess Louise (Argyll and Sutherland Highlanders) attached to 1/6th. (Renfrewshire) Battn. of the same Regiment. 2nd. Lieutenant Edward Alexander McKenzie: Military Cross. 2. 1/6th. (Renfrewshire) Battn. Princess Louise (Argyll and Sutherland Highlanders) T.F. Lieutenant (Temp. Captain) David Nelson Bay Robertson: Military Cross.	

WAR DIARY
or
INTELLIGENCE SUMMARY

Army Form C. 2118

1/10th A.I.S. Highrs

Page 5

Place	Date	Hour	Summary of Events and Information	Remarks and references to Appendices
Labyrinth Sector M.2.	19/4/16		2. The above named Officers displayed great gallantry and initiative when the enemy exploded two mines in front of our parapet.	
			3. No. 2091, Private James Flynn: Distinguished Conduct Medal.	
			4. No. 3019, Pte. (Lance Corpl.) Andrew Wilson	
			5. No. 1445, Pte. (Lance Corpl.) Alexander Wilson } Military Medal.	
			6. No. 79, Private John McPhail	
			The above named N.C.Os. and men distinguished themselves on the 31st March 1916, when the enemy exploded two mines under our trenches. Pte. Flynn by his prompt action and courage in bombing the enemy out of the sap and crater. Lce Corpl. Andrew Wilson in restoring communication between the Left Coy. and Battn. H.Q.; Lce. Corpl. Alexander Wilson in bombing the enemy out of the Trench with Sergeant Myron of the same unit (Who was killed in this action); Pte. McPhail by his courageous devotion and disregard for his own personal safety as a stretcher bearer.	
			(51st D. R.O. No. 494, para. 1)	
			The Brigadier tenders to all the above mentioned Officers, N.C.Os. and men his warmest congratulations on their well earned honours.	
	20/4/16		Enemy active during forenoon and again from 3:30 to 5:30pm with artillery fire, oileans, and aerial torpedoes. All damage repaired during the night. From 10pm. till midnight enemy snipers active but on our snipers replying with vigour, enemy ceased for the night.	
	21/4/16		Enemy quiet except for usual sniping activity. Our Trench mortar (2") firing at 16.a.95.03. caused a big explosion, showing planks and mud high into the air. Big cordeys smoke was caused. This point is located and probably a store of oil cans was exploded	

WAR DIARY
or
INTELLIGENCE SUMMARY
(Erase heading not required.)

Army Form C. 2118

1/6th Arg & Suthd. Highrs.

Place	Date	Hour	Summary of Events and Information	Remarks and references to Appendices
Sector M.2.	22/4/16		Official intimation received that following decorations have been granted:-	
			Date of Award. 21st April 1916.	
			2nd. Lieut. J. M. Caldwell. Military Cross.	
			This officer, on 10/4/16, when a mine was exploded by the enemy worked his way forward to a party of his men who had been isolated, taking with him one man and a sack of grenades. The task was extremely difficult and dangerous, it being daylight and the ground being within 65 yards of the enemy.	
			No. 367. Sgt. John McRae. Military Medal.	
			This N.C.O. was in charge of the party mentioned above which had been cut off. This party which was within 25 yards of an enemy sap, remained to rescue one man who had been buried.	
			Battalion relieved by 8th. Argylls. Relief completed by 6.15 p.m. Battalion in Divisional Reserve. Working parties found for R.E. at Railway Station. Bathing of men completed.	
MARJEUIL	23/4/16		Battalion in Divisional Reserve.	
	24/4/16		At 5 p.m. the ceremony of pinning medal ribbons on recipients of decorations was carried out by G.O.C. 51st. (H) Divisn. Battalion marched to HAUTE AVESNES where ceremony took place. Tea was provided and after the parade a special performance was held in the Divisional Theatre to which recipients of decorations and 150 men per battalion were invited.	
			Battalion relieved 6th. Seaforths in Brigade Reserve at ARIANE.	
ARIANE	25/4/16 26/4/16		Battalion in Brigade Reserve. 325 men per day found for work under R.E. for guards, police etc.	Appx. 2a

WAR DIARY or INTELLIGENCE-SUMMARY

1/6. A. & S. Hghrs.

Army Form C. 2118
Page 7

Place	Date	Hour	Summary of Events and Information	Remarks and references to Appendices
ARIANE	27/4/16		Battalion in Brigade Reserve. A.& S. Coy. in support trenches at CHEMIN CREUX. B. & D. Coys. in Reserve at ARIANE. Operation order issued arranging for relief of 1/5th Argylls in M.2 Sector	
ARIANE	28/4/16	2:10am	Enemy exploded 4 mines in sector (M.N.) Heavy bombardment of fire and support trenches wounding 5 of our men. Battalion stood to arms till day break but was not required to reinforce front line. During the absence of Lieut. Col. R.J. Rawson on special leave from 20/4/16 to 9/5/16, command of battalion was taken over temporarily by Captain N.E. Orr 1/5th Seaforth Hghrs. Major R.A.B. Haldane granted leave of absence from 25/4/16 pending release for munition work at home. Battalion relieved 1/8th Argylls.	
(Ref. Trench Map. 51B.N.W.1. 1/10000) A.16.d.	29/4/16		Battalion in Front Line Trenches. Situation generally quiet, except for occasional trench mortar and artillery activity.	
"	30/4/16		Battalion in Front Line Trenches. Situation quiet during day. A statement of strength, increase and decrease, casualties, honors and rewards etc. is attached as an appendix.	Appendix 3.

N. E. Orr Captain
Commanding, 1/6th. A.& S.H.

Territorial Force Association of the County of Renfrew.

Telegrams: "Territorial, Paisley."
Telephone No. 707.

Secretary:
Capt. J. W. Smith-Neill.

13 ST. JAMES PLACE,
PAISLEY.

31st March, 1916.

Appendix T

The Officer Commanding.,
  1/6th Batt. Arg. & Suthd. Highrs.,
    British Expeditionary Force,
      F R A N C E.

38 Millbrae Crescent
Langside.

Answered 31/3/16
NMS

I enclose letter, and excerpt referred to, addressed to you by Messrs. Keyden Strang & Coy, Solicitors, Glasgow, intimating a bequest of £100, less legacy duty at 10%, by Mrs. Jane Hamilton to the Colonel, for the time being, of the 1/6th Battalion Argyll and Sutherland Highlanders, for behoof of disabled or partially disabled soldiers born in, or associated with, the town of Renfrew.

In informing Messrs. Keyden & Coy. that I would forward the letter to you, and that as you would probably not be in the district during the progress of the War, you might, after accepting the legacy, wish to depute the disposal of it to someone who is in touch with such soldiers after they are sent home.

In a further letter, they say that they will require a discharge from you in exchange for payment of the money, and ask if they will send this to me to forward to you for signature when they are in a position to make payment. They say that they do not think that their clients would object to you deputing the disposal of it anyone, but they would like to know that it would be dealt with by someone in a position to make good use of it

Huldledge CAPTAIN
Acting Secretary,
R. T. F. A.

COPY NO. 1
Office
Appendix 2

OPERATION ORDER NO.4 BY LIEUT.COL.R.I.RAWSON,
COMMANDING, 1/6th.BATTN.ARG.& SUTH'D.HIGHRS.
15th.April, 1916.

1 RELIEFS.
1/6th. Argylls ~~will relieve xxxx~~ and 51st. Div. Cyclist Coy. will relieve 1/8th.Argylls in M.2. Sector on 16th.inst as follows.
Reliefs will be from Left to Right.

2 "A" & "B" COYS.
"A" & "B" Coys. Will move off by Platoons at 1-30p.m. via ANZIN- MADAGASCAR-BOYAU DE LA VASE and will relieve Left Coy.1/8th.Argylls.

3 "C" & "D" COYS.
"C" & "D" Coys. will move off by Platoons using above route and will relieve Right Coy., 1/8th.Argylls. Move off at 2p.m.from MAROEUIL.

4 CYCLIST COMPANY.
51st.Div. Cyclist Company will move off at 2-30p.m. using above route and will take over support trenches from 1/8th.Argylls.in vicinity of Point 777 and BOYAU DE LA VASE.

5 GUIDES.
The four H.Q. Company Guides will accompany the Cyclist Company and will guide them into position in Support Trenches.
Guides will report to the Regtl. Serjt.Major at 2-15p.m.

6 SIGNALLERS.
Signallers will move off under the Signalling Officer at 12 noon.

7 LEWIS DETACHMENT.
Lewis Detachment, under 2/Lieut.J.H.E.Coats,will move off at 10a.m.

8 BOMBERS.
Battalion Bombers,under 2/Lieut.P.Harrington,will move off along with Signallers at 12 noon.

9 SNIPERS.
Snipers,under Lieut.L.L.Shearer,will move off along with Signallers at 12 noon and will take over all sniping posts ,sniperscopes etc.,and will learn all they can about the enemy's line.

10 H.Q.DETAILS.
H.Q.Details, under the Regtl.Serjt.Major,will move off at 3p.m. The Regtl.Serjt.Major will take over all Trench Stores at Battn.H.Q.

11 TRENCH STORES-OFICERS & N.C.O,s TAKING OVER.
One Officer and 4 N.C.O,s per Company will leave MAROEUIL at 12-30p.m. and proceed to Trenches to take over Trench Stores etc. Duplicate Lists of Trench Stores will be forwarded to Battn.H.Q. by 8p.m.

12 DINNERS-WATER BOTTLES-S.A.A.
Companies and Specialists will have dinners before moving off. Water Bottles will be filled and all men completed to 120 rounds S.A.A.

13 BILLETS.
Billets will be left thoroughly clean.

14 BAGGAGE.
All Baggage and Mess Baskets required for Trenches will be handed over to the Qr.Mr. ,clearly labelled,before moving off. Baggage will be brought to railhead on trucks,arriving about 8p.m.

15 BATTN.H.Q.
Battn.H.Q. will arrive at 5p.m.

16 REPORTS.
Reports to Battn H.Q. when relief is completed.

Captain,
Adjt., 1/6th.A. &S. Highrs.

DISTRIBUTION.

Copy No.	1	Filed	Copy No.	7	Signallers.
" "	2	O.C. A Coy.	" "	8	O.C. Cyclist Coy.
" "	3	O.C. B Coy.	" "	9	Sniping Officer.
" "	4	O.C. C. Coy.	" "	10	Qr.Mr. & Trans.Offr.
" "	5	O.C. D. Coy.	" "	11	A/Bde.H.Q.
" "	6	O.C.Lewis Det.	" "	12	O.C. 1/8th.Argylls.

War Diary   Appendix 2(a)

Secret

Copy No. 1

OPERATION ORDER BY CAPTAIN, N.C. ORR,

COMMANDING 1/6th. BATTN. ARG. & SUTH'D. HIGHRS.

24th. April, 1916.

(1) The Battalion will relieve 1/6th. Bn. Seaforths to-morrow, 25th. inst. in Support Trenches.

(2) A & B. Coys. (formed as one Coy.) will parade at 2 p.m. and march by Platoons via ANZIN & ARIANE taking over shelters on right of CHEMIN CREUX. This Coy. will act as Support Coy. to 6th. Seaforths.
C. Coy. will parade at 2-30 p.m. and follow A & B. Coys. taking over shelters on left of CHEMIN CREUX and will act as Supporting Coy. to 8th. Argylls.
D. Coy. will follow C. Coy. and take over shelters at ARIANE.

(3) The Lewis Detachment and Signalling Section will parade at 12 noon and take over positions in Support Trenches.

(4) Headquarter Details under Lieut. A. Lang will parade at 3 p.m.

(5) All Officers baggage for Trenches will be stacked at Quartermasters Store by 2 p.m.

(6) O.C. Coys. will send up 1 Officer per Coy. at 12-30 p.m. to take over Shelters and Trench Stores in their respective sectors

(7) All baggage left behind will be stacked properly labelled at Quartermasters Store by 12 noon.

(8) Major R Stewart will hand over billets to 6th. Seaforths. O.C. Coys. will render to him a certificate before marching off that all the billets have been left clean.

Captain,

24-4-16.   Adjutant 1/6th. Bn. Arg. &. Suth'd. Hrs.

Distribution.

Copy No. 1   Filed.   Copy No. 7 Signalling Officer.
"   " 2   O.C. A. Coy.   Copy No. 8 Medical Officer.
"   " 3   O.C. B. Coy.   "   "   9 Quartermaster.
"   " 4   O.C. C. Coy.   "   " 10 O.C. 1/6th. Bn.
"   " 5   O.C. D. Coy.   Seaforth Highrs.
"   " 6   O.C. Lewis
              Detachment.

Appendix 3

1/6th Battn. Arg. & Suth'd. Highrs.

Summary of Wastage and Reinforcements - Other Ranks
1/5/15 – 30/4/16.

Wastage	Other Ranks.	Reinforcements.	Other Ranks.
Killed.	86.	Embarkation Strength.	990.
Wounded (Invalided)	196.	Drafts Received:-	
Missing.	20.	June, 1915.	80.
Sick (Invalided)	182.	Nov., 1915.	112.
Discharged.	24.	Feb., 1916.	50.
Transferred to R.E.	13.	Mar., 1916.	50.
Munition Workers.	32.	April, 1916.	50.
Physically Unfit.	12.		
Total.	565.		1332.
Presently serving in France	767		

Distribution of Other Ranks serving in France.
29/4/16

Distribution	Other Ranks.
Available for Trenches.	429
Transport and Details.	77
Detached. (Bde. & Div. Employ etc.)	83.
Sick in Field. Amb. & Con. Coy.	88
Others in Country.	90

CAPTAIN.
ADJT. 6TH ARG. & SUTHND HIGHLRS

1/6th. Battn. Arg. & Suth'd. Highrs.

Statement of Casualties, Admissions to and Discharges from Hospital.

1/5/15 - 30/4/16.

Casualties and Sick		Ultimate Disposal	
Killed.	86.		
Wounded.	242.		
		Returned to Duty	35.
		At Base or in Hospital,	11
		Invalided to England,	196.
			242.
Missing	20.		
Sick to Field Amb.	977		
		Returned to Duty,	632
		In Field Amb. or Con. Company,	89
		At Base or in Hospital,	74
		Invalided to England,	182
			977

_____ CAPTAIN.
ADJT. 6TH ARG. & SUTHND HIGHRS

From 1-5-15 to 30-4-16 LIST OF OFFICERS 1-6TH BN. A & S.H.

KILLED, WOUNDED, INVALIDED OR SECONDED TO OTHER UNITS.

Rank	Name		Casualty	Date
Lt. Col.	Stewart,	J.S.	Invalided	25-9-15
Major	Hepburn,	W.K.	Do	13-8-15
"	Haldane,	R.H.B	Munitions	26-4-16
Capt.	Locke,	H.K.	Invalided	20-12-15
"	Swan,	J.H.C.	Do	23-9-15
"	McLardie,	J.	Do	24-7-15
"	McRobert,	J	Wounded	30-8-15
"	Lang,	F.M.	Killed	18-12-15
Lieut.	Clement,	A.M.	Invalided	13-10-15
"	Milne,	R.S	Do	25-8-15
"	Gardner,	C.	Do	8-11-15 R.D.
2-Lieut.	Lang,	J.O.	Wounded	30-8-15
"	Shanks,	R.J.	Do	25-3-16
"	Hurst,	J.D.	Invalided	16-8-15 R.D.
"	Brown,	W.A.S	R.F.C.	8-3-16
"	Allan,	D.S.	Invalided	5-8-15
"	Forsyth,	W.	Killed	1-4-16
"	McKechnie,	E.A.	11th A & S.H.	18-3-16
"	Ritchie,	J.	Invalided	14-2-16
"	McNeil,	A.	Killed	25-3-16
Capt & Adjt.	Watson,	J.	Invalided	7-6-15
Lt & Qr. Mr.	Thomson,	J.	Do	28-7-15
Capt.	Hardie,	S.J.L	Seconded to 152nd. Bde. M.G. Coy.	16-1-16
Lieut.	Drybrough,	D.N.	Do	Do
"	Shanks,	A	Do	Do

_____ CAPTAIN.
ADJT. 6TH ARG. & SUTHND HIGHRS

1-6TH BN. ARG & SUTH'D. HIGHRS.

OFFICERS & OTHER RANKS DECORATED.

From 1-5-15 to 30-4-16.

REGTL No.	RANK	NAME	COY	DECORATION OR AWARD
	PIPER	CARLYLE, W.	B	DESPATCHES
	LT. COL.	RAWSON, R.I.	A	DO
	L-CPL.	MUIR, W.S.	C	D.C.M.
	CAPT.	ROBERTSON, D.N.	A	MILITARY CROSS
	2-LIEUT.	McKECHNIE, E.A.	A	DO.
	3RD. A & S. H ATT 1-6TH. A & S. H.			
2091	PTE.	FLYNN, J.	D	D.C.M.
3019	L-CPL.	WILSON, A	D	MILITARY MEDAL
79	PTE.	McPHAIL, J.	B	DO.
1645	PTE.	WILSON, A.	A	DO
	2-LIEUT	CALDWELL, J.M.	D	MILITARY CROSS.
367	SERGT	MacRAE, J.	D	MILITARY MEDAL

_____ CAPTAIN.
ADJT. 6TH ARG. & SUTHND HIGHRS

1-6TH. BN. A.& S. H.

COURTS MARTIAL — CONVICTIONS.

From 1-5-15 to 30-4-16.

Nature of Offence.	No. of Convictions.
Drunk.	3.
Sleeping on Post.	8.
Deserting Post.	1.
Absence.	1.
Striking Superior Officer.	1.
Disobeying Orders.	2. (M.G. Coy)
Self Inflicted Wounds.	1.
Total.	17.

_____ CAPTAIN.
ADJT. 6TH ARG. & SUTHND HIGHRS

152nd Bde. SECRET No. 134.

WAR DIARY
of
1/6th Bn. Argyll and Sutherland Highlanders.

From

1st May, 1916.

To.

31st May, 1916.

CONFIDENTIAL

WAR DIARY

of

1/6th. BN. ARG. & SUTH'D. HIGHRS.

from

1 - 5 - 16.   to   31 - 5 - 16.

152nd Infantry Brigade SECRET No. 134.

Headquarters,
 152nd Infantry Brigade.

I send herewith War Diary for month of May, 1916,
for Battalion under my Command.

[signature] Lieut. Colonel,
Commanding 1/6 th Bn. Seaforth Highrs.

2nd June, 1916.

Army Form C. 2118.

WAR DIARY or INTELLIGENCE SUMMARY

(Erase heading not required.)

1/6th. A. & S. Highrs.

Volume XV
Page 1

Place	Date	Hour	Summary of Events and Information	Remarks and references to Appendices
A.16.d. (Ref. French Map 51B. N.W.1, 1/10000)	1/5/16	—	Battalion in Front Line Trenches. Situation quiet.	
	2/5/16	—	Battalion in Front Line Trenches. Slight enemy Trench Mortar and Artillery Activity.	
	3/5/16	—	Battalion in Front Line Trenches. Operation Order issued ordering relief.	
	4/5/16	—	Battalion relieved by 1/8th. Argylls and proceeded to Brigade Reserve. Battn. H.Q. and A.&B. Coys. at Post Ariane. C.&D. Coys. in Support Line	
Ariane	5/5/16	—	Battalion in Brigade Reserve, 120 men found for R.E. Working Parties	
"	6/5/16	—	Battalion in Brigade Reserve. 120 men found for R.E. Working Parties	
"	7/5/16	—	Battalion in Brigade Reserve. 120 men found for R.E. Working Parties. Operation order issued for move to MARJEUIL.	
MARJEUIL	8/5/16	—	Battalion relieved by 1/8th. Seaforth and proceeded to Billets in Divisional Reserve at MARJEUIL.	
"	9/5/16	—	Battalion in Divisional Reserve. Bathing and cleaning up. 100 men found for R.E. Working Party.	
"	10/5/16	—	Battalion in Divisional Reserve. 100 men found for R.E. working Party. Operation orders issued for relief of 1/8 L.L. Argylls in M.L. Sector.	
A.16.d. (Ref. French Map 51B. N.W.1. 1/10000)	11/5/16	—	Relief of 1/8th. Argylls completed by 5-45 p.m. Working Party heard near A.16.a.9.2. (Ref. French Map) was dispersed by our Lewis Gun fire. Remainder of the night was quiet.	
	12/5/16	—	Battalion in Front Line Trenches. Situation generally quiet. 2/Lieut. A.L. Paterson joined Battalion for duty.	
	13/5/16	—	Battalion in Front Line Trenches. Situation quiet	
	14/5/16	—	Battalion in Front Line Trenches. Enemy inactive during forenoon. In afternoon slight mortar and grenade activity damaging our trenches in places.	

Army Form C. 2118.

WAR DIARY
or
INTELLIGENCE SUMMARY

(Erase heading not required.)

1/6th A. & S. Highrs.

Page 2

Place	Date	Hour	Summary of Events and Information	Remarks and references to Appendices
A.16.d. (Ref French Map 57B N.W.1. 1/10000.)	15/5/16		Battalion in Fire Trenches. Situation quiet. Draft of 62 other ranks of 8th A.& S.H. attached to Battalion and posted to companies.	
	16/5/16		Battalion in Fire Trenches. Situation quiet.	
	17/5/16		Battalion in Fire Trenches. Situation quiet. Operation Order for relief issued.	
			Battalion relieved by 1/8th Argylls. Relief completed by 6 p.m. Battalion in Brigade Reserve at ARIANE.	
ARIANE	18/5/16		Battalion in Brigade Reserve. Working parties found for work under R.E.	
"	19/5/16		Battalion in Brigade Reserve. Working parties found for work under R.E.	
"	20/5/16		Battalion in Brigade Reserve. Working parties found for work under R.E.	
"	21/5/16		Battalion in Brigade Reserve. Working parties found for work under R.E.	
"	22/5/16		Battalion in Brigade Reserve. Working parties found for work under R.E.	
"	23/5/16		Battalion in Brigade Reserve. Operation Order No. 9 issued for move to Rest Billets at AGNIÈRES and CAPELLE FREMONT (Ref. sheet 51C. 1/40000 E.2.C & D)	
AGNIÈRES	24/5/16		Battalion in Rest Billets. Cleaning up, washing, kit inspections etc.	
"	25/5/16		Battalion in Rest Billets. Training of Companies, Lewis Detachment, Bombers etc.	
"	26/5/16		Battalion in Rest Billets. Training etc. as usual.	
"	27/5/16		Battalion in Rest Billets. Training etc. as usual.	
"	28/5/16		Battalion in Rest Billets. Church Parades and inspection of last two drafts by G.O.C. 152 Inf. Bde.	

WAR DIARY or INTELLIGENCE SUMMARY

Army Form C. 2118.

1/6th Bn. Arg. & Suthd. Highrs.

Page 3.

Place	Date	Hour	Summary of Events and Information	Remarks and references to Appendices
AGNIÈRES	29/5/16		Battalion in Rest Billets. Training of companies and specialists.	
"	30/5/16		Battalion in Rest Billets. Order received for Battalion to proceed to ARRAS to join 51st Division as a Pioneer Battalion. Move to take place 6 pm. 31st. A large number of men in convalescent Coy. and employed throughout the Division were returned to Battalion prior to move.	
	31/5/16	10 am	Battalion in Rest Billets. Order for move postponed meantime. Battalion to stand fast in present Billets till relieved to move by 51st Division.	Appendices: 1 Strength, Casualties and sick. 2 List of Officers. 3 Copies of Operation Orders

LIEUT COL.
O/C. 1/6th ARG. & SUTH'D HIGH'S.

Appendix. 1

1/6th. Bn. Arg. & SUTH'D. HIGHRS.

STATEMENT OF CASUALTIES, ADMISSIONS TO AND DISCHARGES FROM HOSPITAL.

WASTAGE.		REINFORCEMENTS.	
Killed.	1.	Fighting Strength 30/4/16,	677.
Wounded.	5.	Draft 1/8th. A. & S. H.	62.
Missing.	-	Draft 11th. A. & S. H.	23.
Sick in Field Amb.	79	Returned from Hospital.	122.
TOTAL.	85.	TOTAL.	884.
Fighting strength, 31/5/16.	799		
TOTAL.	884.		

31st. May, 1916.

_____ Capt.
Adjt. 1/6th. Bn. A. & S. H.

Appendix 2

1/6th. BN. A. & S. H.

LIST OF OFFICERS - 30 - 5 - 16.

RANK.	NAME.	COY.	REMARKS.
Battalion H.Q.			
Lieut. Col.	RAWSON, R.I.	A.	Comdg. Officer. (Glos. Regt.)
Major.	STEWART, R.	B.	Senior Major.
Captain.	COATS, S.	B.	
Captain.	THOMAS, A.G.	B.	Adjutant. (S. Staffs. Regt.)
Lieut. & Q.M.	SCAIFE, J.	A.	Quartermaster.
Lieut.	SHANKS, J.A.G.	D.	Transport Officer.
Lieut.	STOCKDALE, J.H.	A.	Transport Officer.
Lieut.	COATS, J.H.E.	D.	Lewis Detachment.
Captain.	PHILLIPS, W.W.	A.	R.A.M.C. Medical Officer.
A COMPANY.			
Captain.	BROWN, J.H.	A.	O.C. A. Coy.
Lieut.	HARRINGTON, P.	A.	HOSPITAL
2/Lieut.	HURST, J.H.D.	A.	
2/Lieut.	YOUNG, A.G.	A.	
2/Lieut.	MUIR, W.S.	A.	HOSPITAL
B COMPANY.			
Captain.	ROBERTSON, D.N.	B.	O.C. B. Coy.
Lieut.	LANG, A.	B.	
2/Lieut.	McKILLIGAN, W.H.	B.	(1/6th. Sea. Highrs. Att.)
2/Lieut.	McDONALD, J.W.L.T.	B.	
2/Lieut.	BROWN, G.S.	B.	HOSPITAL.
C COMPANY.			
Captain.	CRAIG, A.	C.	O.C. C. Coy.
Lieut.	SHEARER, L.L.	C.	
2/Lieut.	BROWN, R.A.	C.	Intell., Snpg., & Bilt. Offr.
2/Lieut.	SMELLIE, W.T.	C.	Signalling Officer.
2/Lieut.	PIRIE, G.J.	C.	
2/Lieut.	NAIRN, A.	C.	Act. L.D. Officer.
Lieut	GARDNER, C	C	O.C. D COY.
D COMPANY.			
Captain.	McHAFFIE, H.McC.	D.	AT BASE DEPOT
Lieut.	SHANKS, W.	D.	152nd. Bde. Gren. Officer.
2/Lieut.	LOVE, D.A.	D.	
2/Lieut.	COATS, C.W.	D.	Bombing Officer. HOSPITAL
2/Lieut.	CALDWELL, J.M.	D.	HOSPITAL.
2/Lieut.	MUIR, N.M.	D.	
2/Lieut.	SHEARER, A.	D.	(1/9th. A. & S. H. Att.)

RANK.	NAME.	COY.	REMARKS.
Captain.	PATON, J.S.	B.	Off strength. Sick leave to SCOTLAND.
2/Lieut.	PATERSON, A.L.		Employed 152nd. Bde. Staff.
2/Lieut.	MARTIN, C.		1/9th. A. & S. H. Base Depot.
2/Lieut.	FARQUHARSON, C.		do.
2/Lieut.	BONAR, G.N.		do.

Fighting Strength.	32
Officers present with Battn.	22
Officers sick.	5.
Officers on leave.	3.
Extra regimentally employed.	1.
Posted but not joined.	4.
Sick in SCOTLAND.	1.

_____ CAPTAIN.
ADJT. 6TH ARG. & SUTHND HIGH^{DS}

War Diary *Secret* *Copy No 1*

Appendix 3

OPERATION ORDER BY,

    CAPTAIN, N.C. ORR,

      COMMANDING 1/6th. BATTN. ARG. &. SUTH'D. HIGHRS.

        10th. May, 1916.

1. RELIEF.   The Battalion will relieve 1/8th. Bn. Arg. &. Suth'd. Highrs. in M.2. Sub-Sector to-morrow, 11th. May, 1916.

2. BOUNDARY.   The Boundary between M.1. and M.2. is now the Sap running up to Crater at 277 which will be held by Battn. in M.1. Sub-Sector.

3. COYS.   C. &. D. Coys. made up in 8 Platoons will relieve Right front Coy. leading Platoon to pass ARAINE at 3-30 p.m. and will move via VASE & ~~VICTORIA STREET~~ dropping 3 Platoons in Support Trench to relieve ~~Right~~ Support Coy. Frontage of this ~~this~~ Coy. will be from Sap at 277 exclusive to D. exclusive.
VASE-VICTORIE RIGHT

A. &. B. Coys. made up in 8 Platoons will relieve Left front Coy. moving off after C. &. D. Coys. are clear and proceed via VASE ~~VICTORIE~~ dropping 3 Platoons in Support Trench to relieve Left Support Coy. Frontage of Coy. will be from D. inclusive to present Left of Sub-Sector.
VASE-BAIRD ST

Lewis Gun Detachment will relieve 1/8th. Bn. A. &. S. H. at 2 p.m.

Signallers will relieve 1/8th. Bn. A. &. S. H. at 2-15 p.m.

Snipers and Battn. Bombers will report at Battn. Hqrs. at M.2. Sub-Sector at 2-30 p.m. and take over from 1/8th. Bn. Arg. &. Suth'd. Highrs.

4. TRENCH STORES.
    One Officer per Coy. and 1 Officer from C. D. Coys. (to take over stores in Support Line) will report at Battn. Hqrs. in M.2. Sub-Sector at 2 p.m. to take over stores etc.

5. WATER BOTTLES.
    Water Bottles must be taken into Trenches filled.

                                                Lieut.,

Issued at 3 p.m.   Act. Adjutant 1/6th. Bn. A. &. S. H.

                DISTRIBUTION.

Copy. No. 1. Retained.
Copy. No. 2. by Orderly to O.C. 1/8th. Bn. A. &. S. H.
Copy. No. 3. -6   O.C. Coys.
Copy. No. 7. Signalling Officer.
Copy. No. 8. Bombing Officer.
Copy. No. 9. Lewis Gun Officer.
Copy. No. 10. Quartermaster.
Copy. No. 11. Transport Officer.

SECRET.   Copy no. 1

Operation Order No. 8.
by Lieut. Col. R.J. Rawson, commanding 1/6th A&SH
                                17th. May, 1916

1. RELIEF

The Battalion will relieve the 1/5-th. Sea. Highrs. in Brigade Reserve to-day, 17th. May.

B. Coy. will relieve the company at Hd. Qrs. ARIANE; A. Coy. 2 platoons at ARIANE and 2 platoons in VASE TRENCH; C. Coy. in CHEMIN CREUX on the right; D. Coy. in CHEMIN CREUX on the left.

2. COMPANIES

Coys. will be relieved by Coys. of 1/8th. Argylls as follows:—

B. Coy. will relieve Right Front Coy. D. Coy. Left Front Coy. C. Coy. will come into Right Support and A. Coy. to Left Support.

3. MEALS

Dinners will be as usual. Teas will be prepared in hot food containers and taken to the new Company H.S. before 4 p.m. Containers will be cleaned under supervision of the Sergt. Cook (Acting) before being handed over to the 1/8 th. Argylls and must therefore be returned to the cookhouse directly after the tea is issued.

4. BAGGAGE
Cooking pots and all cookhouse baggage will be stacked at ARIANE ready for the Transport, as detailed by the Regtl. Sergt. Major.

5 ROUTES
On relief the right company will move out via ARGYLL ST. & Baird Street and DOUAI AVENUE
Platoons in support will follow their own companies as they move out.

6 QUARTERS - TRENCH STORES
1 Officer & 1 NCO per coy. will take over quarters from 5th. Seaforths at 10am taking over any trench stores.

7 SANITATION
The Lines and Dug-outs must be left perfectly clean

                        Haug Lieut.
Issued at 10ar   act. Adjt. 1/6 Cd. A & H.
Copy No 1 Files.
" " 2/5 O.C. Coys
" " 6 L.D.
" " 7 Sigs
" " 8 Bombers
" " 9 Sergt book
" " 10 QM. & T.O.

War Diary   Copy No 1

Operation Order No. 9.
                by
Lieut. Col. R.S. Rawson, Comdg. 1/6th. Q.T.S.H.
                    23/5/16

___

1. MOVE
The Battalion will move to Rest Billets at
AGNIERES and CAPELLE FREMONT to-day.
Companies will move off as follows via ANZIN
and MAROEUIL.
B. Coy. at 6.30pm, A. Coy at 6.40 pm. D Coy from
CHEMIN CREUX via VASE Trench at 6-15pm. C
Coy. on relief by a company of 4th. Gordon
Highrs. by the VASE Trench in rear of D Coy
After leaving the Communication Trench at ANZIN
companies will move by Platoons at 200X
distance.
Lewis Detachment with their rifles and equip-
ment will be at ARIANE at 8 pm ready to
load on to the limber wagons and will
escort the transport to billets.
All H.Q. Details will march with their Coys
Officers Messes will send what is necessary
for a meal on arrival, to ANZIN where the
mess cart will be at 6 pm. 1 Officer's servant
per Battn. H.Q. and Coy. will proceed with
the mess cart to Billets.

2. TRENCH STORES.
All Trench Stores on Coy. and Battn. charge
will be handed over to 4th Gordon

2

Nights, except D. Coy S.A.A. which will be handed into Bde. Store at CHEMIN CREUX and Lewis Detachments S.A.A. which will be handed into 1/8th Argylls Battn. Reserve Store. Other Trench Stores of the Lewis Detachment will be brought to Bde. H.Q. at ARIANE and handed over to the Acting Staff Captain before 5:30 pm.

3. ROUTE
Route to be followed will be detailed to Officers later

4. MEALS
Arrangements are being made for the cookers to meet the Battn. en route and if possible, hot drinks will be provided. Dinners and teas will be as usual.

5. BAGGAGE
All baggage will be stacked at ARIANE Dump by 4.30 pm. ready for the Transport and 1 man per Coy. and Battn. H.Q. will remain in charge.
The Signal Officer will detach one NCO to proceed with party. The Pioneer Sergeant will be in charge of the party

6. OFFICERS' HORSES
Officers' Horses to be at a convenient spot on the MAROEUIL – ANZIN Road at 7 pm.

3

7 SHELTERS.
All shelters, trenches, latrines etc to be perfectly clean and certificates obtained by O.C "C" Coy. from 4th. Gordons. All other Coys. and H.Q. Details will render certificates to Battn. H.Q that this order has been obeyed.

8 DRESS.
All ranks must be properly dressed and equipped. Helmets will be worn

                                     Maury Lieut,
23/5/16   Act. Adjt. 1/6 A&SH

Issued at 2pm
   Copy No. 1 Retained
   "   " 2/5 O.C. Coys
   "   " 6 Lewis Det.
   "   " 7 Signallers
   "   " 8 Q.M. & T.O.

Volume XVI.

Vol 14

51

14.N.

Became Pioneers
5th –
12/6/16.

CONFIDENTIAL

WAR DIARY

OF

1/6th. BN. ARG. & SUTH'D. HIGHRS.

from

1 - 6 - 16   to   30 - 6 - 16.

WAR DIARY or INTELLIGENCE SUMMARY

Army Form C. 2118.

Volume XV

1/6th Argt. & Suthd. Highrs. Page 1.

Place	Date	Hour	Summary of Events and Information	Remarks and references to Appendices
Pol Lens II. AGNIERES.	1/6/16		Battalion in Rest Billets. Training of companies and specialists from midnight 1/2nd June. Battalion ceased to belong to 152nd. Infantry Brigade, becoming Divisional Troops. The Battalion came under the direct orders of Headquarters, 51st. Division from this date for Administrative Purposes.	App. I.
"	2/6/16		Battalion in Rest Billets.	
BOIS DES ALLEUX.		6 p.m.	Move to BOIS DES ALLEUX in accordance with instructions from 51st.(H) Division. Battalion lodges in huts in the wood.	
		10-10 p.m.	Order received for 2 Coy. to move to NEUVILLE ST VAST and 2 Coy. to 6.25 (ref. 36c. S.W. 1/20000 sheet) 51E (approx.) Battalion Headquarters to be moved at discretion of S.O.B., 152nd. Inf. Bde.	
"	3/6/16		Major R. STEWART appointed Senr. Major. NEUVILLE ST VAST. Duties assumed by him 3/6/16.	
		8 p.m.	Companies moved off by platoons to take up positions as ordered in 2nd. trail. Battalion Headquarters remain at BOIS DES ALLEUX for the present.	
Ref. SHR.N.W.I. A.2.6. (Near LA TARGETTE)	4/6/16 5/6/16.	8 p.m.	Battn. H.Q. and "B" Coy. moved off to new position in trenches at A.2.6 (Ref. French map 51E.N.W.I). Battalion engaged in work on new shelters in front and intermediate trenches in sub-sector held by 152nd. Inf. Bde. 8 officers and 470 men employed.	
"	6/6/16		Work on shelters continued. 8 officers and 470 men employed. Work continues during the whole 24 hours, the total number provided being divided into 4 reliefs.	
"	7/6/16		Battalion specially engaged in strengthening front and support line defences, working in 6 hour reliefs day and night on VIMY RIDGE. Location and distribution of H.Q. and Coys. shown on attached table.	App. II.

Army Form C. 2148.

WAR DIARY
or
INTELLIGENCE SUMMARY

(Erase heading not required.)

1/6th Bn. Arg. Y Suthd. Highrs. Page 2.

Place	Date	Hour	Summary of Events and Information	Remarks and references to Appendices
Ref. 51 B.N.W. A.2.6. near LA TARGETTE	8/6/16		Battalion still at work on Defences. 8 officers and 400 men employed on this work.	
	9/6/16		Battalion still at work on Defences. 8 officers and 400 men employed on this work.	
	10/6/16		Battalion still at work on Defences. 8 officers and 400 men employed on this work.	
R/51C. ECOIVRES	11/6/16		Battalion moved to huts at BRAY and ECOIVRES preparatory to joining 5th Division as a Pioneer Battn.	App. III
	12/6/16	11 am	Battalion inspected by G.O.C. 51st Division who delivered a farewell address to the Officers and men prior to their leaving his Division. He thanked them for their good work while under his command and hoped that they would do as well in their new division as they had done under him. He regretted the parting, but would always follow with interest their subsequent career and would constantly inquire after them in their new sphere. The Battalion afterwards marched past in fours. 3 Officers joined for duty from Base Depot.	W.E.
		8.3 pm	Battalion formed up in column of route for march to ARRAS which was reached about 11.30 pm. Billets in RUE BAUDIMONT. Battn. H.Q. in RUE DE CHATEAUDUN. "C" Coy. in LOUEZ. Q.M. Stores & Transport at AGNEZ	App. IV
ARRAS	13/6/16		Battalion in billets in ARRAS. Day spent by companies in making billets as comfortable as possible. One pair of drab slacks per man was issued. There were cut down to make shorts and are to be worn only by working parties and while in trenches. The kilt will still remain the parade and fighting dress of the unit. Adjustments in administration consequent on joining new division carried out	

2449 Wt. W14957/M90 750,000 1/16 J.B.C. & A. Forms/C.2118/12.

WAR DIARY or INTELLIGENCE SUMMARY

Army Form C. 2118.

1/6th Battn. Arg. & Suth'd Highrs.   Page 3.

Place	Date	Hour	Summary of Events and Information	Remarks and references to Appendices
ARRAS.	13/6/16 (cont.)		The companies were placed at disposal of C.R.E., 51st. Division for work on Front Line Defences, each company having its allotted task to perform and working independently. All work is carried out at night.	
"	14/6/16		Companies continue work, programme as arranged with C.R.E.	
"	15/6/16		Companies continue work, programme as arranged with C.R.E.	
"	16/6/16		Companies continue work, programme as arranged with C.R.E.	
"	17/6/16		Companies continue work, programme as arranged with C.R.E. All workshops organised and started on a proper footing. Interior economy generally improved and re-organised to suit present circumstances.	
"	18/6/16		Working parties carried out work as usual, but arrangements made for return of all R.E. stores on company charge.	
"	19/6/16	10-30 p.m.	Operation Order No. 95 for move to LATTRE received. Arrangements for move made.	App. V.
LATTRE.	20/6/16	3 p.m.	Battalion left ARRAS, moving with 1/4 mile intervals between half companies as far as DANVILLE-MARDEUIL Railway (Ref. 1/140,000. Sheets 51B & 51C.) Billets reached 3 a.m. 20th.	
GRAND RULLECOURT.	21/6/16		Battalion formed up ready for move to billets in GRAND RULLECOURT. Arrived 5 km. Battalion in Rest Billets. Cleaning up. Kit inspections etc. One company placed daily at the disposal of	
	22/6/16		O.C. 51st. Div. School for use as training company and for making entanglements, wiring etc. Battalion training by companies under company arrangements. Training programme for remainder of week drawn up and issued to companies. Scheme for collecting stores in case of an advance prepared.	App. VI. App. VII.

Army Form C. 2118.

WAR DIARY
or
INTELLIGENCE SUMMARY
(Erase heading not required.)

1/6th Arg. & Suthd. Highrs.   Page 4

Place	Date	Hour	Summary of Events and Information	Remarks and references to Appendices
GRAND RULLECOURT	23/6/16		Training as per training programme. 2/Lieut. A. NAIRN attached for duty to 95th. Bde. M. G. Company.	
	24/6/16		Training as per training programme. 3 officers joined Battn. for duty from Base Depot, viz: 2/Lieuts. R.C. POLLOCK, W.P. M'CREATH, E. ORR.	
	25/6/16		Church Parades. Half-holiday.	
	26/6/16		Training as per training programme.	
	27/6/16		Training as per training programme.	
	28/6/16		Training as per training programme. Major R.H.B. HALDANE returned from England and joined Battalion for duty.	
	29/6/16		Training as per training programme.	
	30/6/16		Training as per training programme.	
			Appendices:— VIII Strength, Casualties and Sick. IX List of Officers	

M. Munro
LIEUT.-COL.
CMDG. 6TH ARG. & SUTHD. HIGHRS

1/6th BATTN. ARG. & SUTH'D. HIGHRS.

WAR DIARY - JUNE 1916.

APPENDIX 1.

Orders relative to change in
character of Battalion.

Appendix II

Map Reference:- Combined
Trench Map VIMY, 1/20000

To 51st Divn.

With reference to your signal message A.205 d/4/6/16, strength of the information requested.

	OFFICERS	O.R.	MAP LOCATION	NAME OF TRENCH
Headquarters 1 Platoon A.Coy.	4 —	22 26	S.26.c.3.2. approx. do	Junction of PONT and PYLLONES.
A.Coy.	5 (1 in Leave) (1 in Hospital)	99	S.25.d.	Junction of PONT ST and the ARRAS-BETHUNE RD.
B.Coy.	4 (1 in Leave)	124	A.9.a.1.8. approx.	DENIS LE ROCK
C.Coy.	6	121	A.3.d.1.1. approx.	DENIS LE ROCK
D.Coy.	6 (1 in Leave) (2 sick)	134	A.3.d.2.5. approx.	COMBOW ST.
Lewis Detachment	1	52	H.Q. at A.9.a.1.8. approx.	Lewis rifles with their teams in Parallel VIII
TOTAL	26	578		

B, C & D Companies & 2 Lewis Detach. are held at the disposal of O.C. NEUVILLE defences.
H.Qrs and A Coy. are held as a reserve under the direct orders of the Brigadier General Commanding 152nd Inf. Bde.

Appendix 2

SECRET Appendix 3

OPERATION ORDER NO. 11.   COPY NO. Spare

BY

LIEUT. COL. R.I. RAWSON, COMMANDING 1/6th. BN. A. & S. H.

11th JUNE, 1916.

---

1. **MOVE.**
   The Battalion will proceed to Billets in Huts at BRAY tonight 11th inst. and will move in order stated and at time stated.

2. **COMPANIES.**
   B. Coy. will pass cross-roads at LA TARGETTE at 9 p.m.
   C. Coy. after B. Coy. at 9-10 p.m.
   D. Coy. after C. Coy. at 9-20 p.m.
   A. Coy. will move off from its present position at 9-20 p.m. and proceed via LA TARGETTE.
   Each Coy. will leave 1 L/Cpl and 2 men to load baggage on to transport.

3. **H.Q. DETAILS.**
   H.Q. Details under the Regtl. Sergt. Major will move off in front of A. Coy.

4. **LEWIS DETACHMENT.**
   Lewis Detachment will have Guns and Baggage ready for Loading on transport at 9-30 p.m. which will be left in charge of a loading party.
   Remainder of Detachment will then move off via LA TARGETTE and move in rear of Battalion.

5. **GENERAL.**
   100 yards will be kept between Platoons.
   Billets and dug-outs will be left clean.
   Guides will meet Companies at cross-roads leading into ST. ELOY.
   Medical Cart will be at B. Coys dump.
   Coy. Officers horses will be on the ST ELOY - NEUVILLE ST VAAST ROAD at the point where the light railway turns into the cutting.
   Hot drinks will be ready on arrival of Battalion.
   Reports will be sent to Headquarters when Companies are settled in Billets.

11th JUNE, 1916.   Captain,
                                      Adjutant 1/6th. Bn. A. & S. H.
DISTRIBUTION.

No. 1 Copy Retained.
No. 2/5 Copies O.C. Coys.
No. 6 Copy H.Q. Details.
No. 7 Copy Lewis Detachment.
No. 8 Copy Medical Officer.
No. 9 Copy Quartermaster and T.O.

SPECIAL ORDER of the DAY

by

Brig. Gen. W. C. Ross, C.B., Comdg. 152nd Inf. Brigade.
==

Sunday, 11th June, 1916.

On the departure of the 1/6th Battalion, Argyll and Sutherland Highlanders from the Brigade, the Brigadier desires to place on Record the excellent service of the Battalion as a Fighting Unit. Since they have assumed Pioneer duties, they have taken that up with equal determination, and it will be a satisfaction to them to know that the good work they have done may result in saving life and limb for many of their comrades.

The Brigadier deeply regrets the necessity for the parting and feels sure that wherever they go, they will continue to reflect credit on the Brigade to which they originally belonged.

T. M. BOOTH, Major,
Brigade Major,
152nd Infantry Brigade.

SECRET.

Nº G.998

1/6th Argyll & Suth'd. Highrs.

51st HIGHLAND DIVISION.

[Stamp: 1/6th BATTALION ARGYLL & SUTHERLAND HIGHLANDERS 13 JUN 1916]

Ref. Map Sheet 51.c. 1/40,000.

1. The 1/6th Argyll & Sutherland Highlanders will be attached to the 5th Division from the 12th inst., as Pioneer Battalion, and will be billeted as follows:-

   H.Q. and 3 Coys.   .. ARRAS.
   1 Company   .. SUCRERIE, LOUEZ.
   Transport   .. AGNEZ-LES-DUISANS.

2. Billeting parties will report to:-

   Town Major, ARRAS, at 10 a.m. on 12th inst.
   Town Comdt. LOUEZ, at 3 p.m. on 12th inst.
   Town Comdt. AGNEZ-LES-DUISANS, at 3 p.m., 12th inst.

3. The Battalion will move via the ST. POL - ARRAS Road as far as Road Junction G.20.b.2.8., where it will turn South and enter ARRAS by the Road from Fbge. D'AMIENS. It will pass the Railway L.9.a.6.0 at 10 p.m. From this point an interval of at least 300 yards will be maintained between Companies.
   Guides from the billeting parties will meet the Companies proceeding to ARRAS at Road Junction G.20.b.2.8.
   The Company proceeding to the SUCRERIE, LOUEZ, will be similarly met at the Railway (L.9.a.6.0) and the transport at the Road Junction (L.1.d.9.8).

4. The attention of the O.C. 1/6th A. & S. Highrs. is directed to Town Orders, ARRAS.

5. Refilling Point, 13th inst., - 12 noon in K.7.d.

6. The Battalion will form part of the 5th Divisional Troops. Administrative correspondence will be forwarded direct to Headquarters, 5th Division.

7. The departure of the Battalion in accordance with the above Order will be telegraphed to H.Q., 51st Division.

                                    Ian Stewart
                                    Lieut.Colonel,
                                    General Staff,
11th June 1916.   51st (Highland) Division.

Copies to:-
152nd Inf. Bde.   "A"
153rd Inf. Bde.   Divl. Train.
154th Inf. Bde.   A.D.M.S.
1/8th Royal Scots.   Signals.
C.R.A.   S.S.O.
C.R.E.   A.P.M.
D.A.D.O.S.

Appendix 5

SECRET.

5th Division Operation Order No. 95.

19th June, 1916.

1. The 5th Division (less Artillery) will be relieved on its front by the 14th Division, and will move into an area of concentration in accordance with the attached table of moves.

2. Commands of Sectors will be handed over as follows;- completion of all reliefs will be reported to Divisional H.Qrs.

    'I' right sub-sector on night of 19th/20th June.
    'I' left   "   "   " " " 20th/21st June.
    'J' Sector   " " " 20th/21st June.
    'K' Sector   " " " 21st/22nd June.

3. The Artillery and Medium Trench Mortar Batteries of the 5th Division remain in line and come under command of the 14th Division. Any necessary readjustments of zones etc. to be arranged between the respective C.R.A's.

4. First line transport of units of 15th and 95th Infantry Brigades will be clear of their present billets by noon on 21st, and will be accommodated with their battalions.

5. Copies of existing Brigade Sector Defence Schemes, trench maps, air photos, log-books, S.A.A., grenades and trench stores, to be taken over by relieving Brigades.
    Lists of stores etc. so handed over to be forwarded to Divisional Headquarters.

6. Tunnelling Companies will continue to work on their present fronts.

7. Billeting representatives of units will report to Town Commandant of villages in which they are allotted billets, at noon on the same day.

8. All further details to be arranged between Brigades concerned.

ACKNOWLEDGE.

                          Lieutenant Colonel,
          General Staff,   5th Division.

Copies to:-	6th Corps.	14th Division.
	51st Division.	C.R.A.
D.A.D.O.S.	5th Sig. Coy.	C.R.E.
5th Division 'Q'.	13th I. Bde.	15th I. Bde.
A.D.V.S.	95th I. Bde.	A.D.M.S.
	Pioneer Bn.	Div. Train.
	A.P.M.	S.S.O.

5th Division.
S.429.

The attached table should be substituted for that issued with 5th Division Operation Order No. 95 of to-day, the latter table being destroyed.

ACKNOWLEDGE.

[signature]
Lt.Colonel,

19/8/1916.   General Staff, 5th Division.

Copies to -

VI Corps.
14th Division.
51st   "
C.R.A.
C.R.E.
5th Signal Co.
13th Inf. Bde.
15th "   "
95th "   "
Pioneer Battn.
A.D.M.S.
Divisional Train.
A.P.M.
S.S.P.
D.A.D.O.S.
A.D.V.S.
5th Division Q.

Table of Reliefs (issued with 5th Division Operation Order No. 95).

Date	Unit	Sector	Relieving Unit	Billeting area	Remarks
Night 19th/20th.	1 Bn. 95th I.Bde.	'I' Sector right and ST.SAUVEUR.	A Bn. 42nd I.Bde.	BERNEVILLE.	Under orders of B.G.C. 95th I.Bde.
	Pioneer Battn.	ARRAS	—	LATTRE.	
Night 20th/21st.	1 Bn. 95th I.Bde.	Support 'I' Sector	A Bn. 43rd I.Bde.	WANQUENTIN.	Under orders of B.G.C. 95th I.Bde.
	M.G.Co. 95th I.Bde.	'I' Sector right and ST.SAUVEUR.	42nd Inf. Bde.	Transport lines	
	1 Bn. (less 1 Co.) 95th 1/2nd M.G.Coy. R.E.	'I' Sector (left)	A Bn. 43rd I.Bde.	WANQUENTIN LOUEZ.	
	1 Bn. 15th I.Bde.	'J' Sector	A Bn. 43rd I.Bde.	AGNEZ.	
	1 Bn. (less ½ Bn. in Redoubt line) 15th Inf. Bde.	'J' Sector	½ Bn. 43rd I.Bde.	LATTRE.	
	Support Bn. 15th Inf. Bde.	'J' Sector.	—	HAUTEVILLE	
	Reserve Bn. 15th Inf. Bde.	AGNEZ.	—	IZEL.	Under orders of 15th Inf. Bde.
	H.Q. 15th I.Bde.	ARRAS	43rd Inf. Bde.	IZEL	
	Pioneer Battn.	LATTRE	—	GRAND RULLECOURT.	To be clear of LATTRE by 4 p.m.
Night 21st/22nd.	H.Q. 95th I.Bde.	ARRAS	—	SIMENCOURT	Under orders of B.G.C. 95th I.Bde.
	1 Bn. 95th I.Bde.	AGNEZ.	—	SIMENCOURT	
	1 Co. 95th I.Bde.	CEMETERY.	A Co. 43rd I.Bde.	WANQUENTIN.	
	M.G.Co. 95th I.Bde.	'I' Sector (left)	43rd Inf. Bde.	SIMENCOURT	

Table of Reliefs (continued).

Date	Unit	Sector	Relieving unit.	Billeting area.	Remarks.
Night 21st/22nd (contd).	M.G.Co. 15th I.Bde.	'J' Sector	43rd Inf. Bde.	AGNEZ	
	½ Bn. (Redoubt line) 15th Inf. Bde.	'J' Sector	43rd Inf. Bde.	HABARCQ.	Under orders of B.G.C. 15th Inf. Bde.
	½ Bn. 15th Inf. Bde.	LATTRE	-	LANIN	
	1 Bn. 15th Inf. Bde.	AGNEZ	-	IZEL	
	H.Q. 13th I.Bde.	ARRAS	41st Inf. Bde.	AGNEZ	
	2½ Bns. 13th I.Bde.	'K' Sector		AGNEZ	Under orders of B.G.C. 13th Inf. Bde.
	½ Support Bn. 13th Inf. Bde.	'K' Sector		GOUVES	
	Reserve Bn. 13th Inf. Bde.	DUISANS		LATTRE.	
Night 22nd/23rd.	Light T.M.Btys. 95th Inf. Bde. 15th Inf. Bde. 13th Inf. Bde.	'I' Sector. 'J' Sector. 'K' Sector.	Light T.M.Btys. of 41st and 43rd Inf. Bdes.	WANQUENTIN. IZEL. AGNEZ.	
	M.G.Co. 15th I.Bde.	AGNEZ	-	IZEL	To be clear of AGNEZ by 4 p.m.
	M.G.Co. 13th I.Bde.	'K' Sector	41st Inf. Bde.	AGNEZ	
	59th Fd.Co. R.E.	'J' Sector	A Co. R.E. 14th Div.	LATTRE.	
	Durham Fd.Co. R.E.	'K' Sector	- do -	HABARCQ.	
	Sec. 15th Fd. Amb.	ARRAS	A Sec. Fd.Amb. 14th Div.	IZEL	
	½ Bn. 15th Inf. Bde.	HABARCQ	-	HANIN	To be clear of HABARCQ by 4 p.m.

SECRET   Copy No.

           95th Inf.Bde. OPERATION ORDER No. 128

                                               19th JUNE 1916.

           Reference 1/40,000 Sheets 51 B and 51 C.
           ----

1.   The 95th Inf.Bde. will be relieved in I SECTOR by 42nd
and 43rd Inf.Bdes. in accordance with attached Relief Table.

2.   1st Line Transport of all units will be clear of their
present billets by noon on 21st and will be accommodated with
their Battalions in the new area.
         Battalion Commanders will issue orders for movement of
their Transport.

3.   (a) The O.C. I/DEVONS will arrange for one Officer from
Battalion H.Q., and one Officer or N.C.O. per platoon to meet
a similar number of Officers of 6/SOMERSET L.I. at Battalion
H.Q. at 11 a.m. on 20th instant and take them round the
trenches.   Guides from Brigade to Battalion H.Q. will be
arranged by Brigade.
         One Officer per Company of 6/SOMERSET L.I. will report
at DEVONS H.Q. at 6.30 p.m. on the 19th inst.   These Officers
will remain in the trenches until the arrival of their
Companies.

      (b) ~~The O.C. I/EAST SURREY Regt. will arrange to send one
Officer from Battalion H.Q. and one Officer from CEMETERY
and RUE des PORTEURS Company to 43rd Inf.Bde.H.Q. at 10.30 a.m.
21st instant to take round representatives of the 10th Bn.
DURHAM L.I.~~ *Cancelled B.M. 322*

      (c) Arrangements for Officers of 5th K.S.L.I. to visit
trenches of Right Battalion will be made by C.O's concerned.

4.   GUIDES
         Commanding Officers will arrange with C.O's of
relieving Battalions and M.G.Company all details regarding
guides for the Relief, i.e., number required, place of meeting,
and time.
         Guides for Transport will also be arranged.

5.   MACHINE GUNS
         All arrangements for relief of guns in accordance
with Table will be made by O.C. 95th Machine Gun Company with
Os.C. 42nd and 43rd Bde. M.G.Coy.

6.   LEWIS GUNS
         Relieve on the afternoon of the day on which Battalion
relief takes place.   Arrangements to be made between
Battalions.
         Detachments march back with their Battalions.

7.   TOBY GUNS
         The guns and ammunition will be left in the line and
handed over to 43rd Inf.Bde TOBY Detachment.
         The Detachment will march to the Rest Area under the
O.C. and will then rejoin their Battalions.

8.   All ammunition, grenades, tools, trench stores,
trench maps, air photos, log books, copies of Defence Schemes,
and Orders for Supporting points will be handed over.
         Reserve rations in ST.SAUVEUR and CEMETERY will be
handed over.
         Lists of Stores handed over to be sent to Staff Capt.
by 4 p.m. day after relief.

O.O. No.128 (Cont'd)   2

9. **MINING FATIGUES**   5th K.S.L.I. will find mining fatigues and carrying parties for I RIGHT from 8 p.m. Shift on 19th inst.

10.   All troops marching out of ARRAS will move with intervals of 1/4 mile between Half companies until clear of DAINVILLE - MOROEUIL Railway.

11. BILLETING PARTIES will report to TOWN COMMANDANTS of their respective villages at Noon on the day fixed for arrival. At WANQUETIN, DEVONS will be in billets, EAST SURREYS men in Huts and Officers in Tents.   Further instructions regarding tents will follow.

12.   The B.G.C. 42nd Infantry Bde. will assume command of I RIGHT SECTOR on completion of relief on night of 19/20th June.
   The B.G.C. 43rd Infantry Bde. will assume command of I LEFT Subsector and Brigade Reserve on completion of relief on night of 20/21st June.

13.   95th Inf.Bde.H.Q. will open at SIMENCOURT at 11 p.m. on 22nd and will close at ARRAS at same hour.

ACKNOWLEDGE.

Issued at:- 2.30 P.M.

D.K.M.Leod
Capt.
Bde. Major.
95th Inf. Bde.

Copies to:-
No. 1 5th Division.
  2 15th Inf. Bde.
  3 42nd Inf. Bde.
  4 43rd Inf. Bde.
  5 1/Devons.
  6 1/E. Surreys
  7 1/D.C.L.I.
  8 12/Gloucesters.
  9 1/6th A. & S. Highlanders.
 10 1/2 Home Counties Field Co. R.E.
 11 Browells Group
 12 Bde. Signalling Officer
 13 95th Bde.M.G.Coy.
 14 New Zealand Tunn.Coy.R.E.
 15 O.C. TOBY Trench Mortar Bty.
 16 95th Trench Mortar Battery.
 17 No. 3 Company Train.
 18 S.C. 95th Inf. Bde.
 19 Staff Capt.
 20 Bde. Major.
 21 Intelligence Officer
 22 War Diary.

TABLE of RELIEFS 95th Inf.Bde. (Issued with O.O.128)

DATE	UNIT	POSITION	RELIEVED BY	BILLET ON COMPLETION OF RELIEF	REMARKS
Night 19/20th	12/Gloucesters	I RIGHT and ST. SAUVEUR	5/Shropshire L.I.	BERMAVILLE	
	1/6th A.& S. Hldrs.	ARRAS	"	LATTRE	No move before 10 p.m.
Night 20/21st	1/Devons	I LEFT	6/Somerset L.I.	VANQUETIN	
	8 guns 95/Bde.M.G.Co.	ST. SAUVEUR and ARRAS	42nd Bde.M.G.Coy.	Transport Lines	Move again on 21/22nd.
	1/2 Home Counties Field Coy.R.E.	ARRAS	-	LOUEZ	To move by day in small parties. To be clear of ARRAS by 8 p.m.
Night 21/22nd	1/D.C.L.I.	AGNEZ	-	SIMENCOURT	To be clear of AGNEZ by 12 noon
	1/E.Surreys.	ARRAS and CEMETERY.	10/Durham L.I. less 2 Coys.	VANQUETIN	Remaining 2 Coys go out with Battalion.
	3 guns 95/Bde.M.G.Co.	CEMETERY and ARRAS Defences	43rd Bde.M.G.Coy.	SIMENCOURT.	
	8 guns 95/Bde.M.G.Co.	Transport Lines	-	SIMENCOURT.	To be clear of Transport lines by 12 noon.
Night 22/23rd	95th T.M.BATTERY.	J Sector and ARRAS	45rd T.M.BATTERY.	VANQUETIN	
	95th TOBY "	I LEFT Sector.	45rd TOBY "	Rejoin Bns.	Guns remain in line.
	95th Inf.Bde.H.Q.	ARRAS	-	SIMENCOURT	Open at 11 p.m. at SIMENCOURT.

SECRET   95th Inf.Bde. B.M. No. 322

The following corrections should be made in 95th Inf.Bde. OPERATION ORDER No. 128 dated 19/6/16.

1. Cancel para 3 (b)

2. Cancel para 13.

3. In table of Reliefs cancel all references to I/E.SURREYS and H.Q. 95th Inf.Bde., and substitute the following.

DATE	UNIT	POSITION	RELIEVED BY	BILLET ON COMPLETION OF RELIEF.	REMARKS
Night 20/21st	I/E.Surreys less 1 Coy.	ARRAS	10/Durham L.I.	WANQUETIN	
Night 21/22nd	1 Coy. I/E.Surreys	CEMETERY	1 Coy. 10/Durham L.I.	WANQUETIN	
	H.Q. 95th. Inf.Bde.	ARRAS	-	SIMENCOURT	Open at 11 p.m. at SIMEN-COURT.

NOTE:- 1 Coy. I/E.SURREYS in CEMETERY will come under orders of O.C. 10th D.L.I. for tactical purposes from completion of relief of H.Q. I/E.SURREYS on night 20/21st till relieved by 10th DURHAM L.I. on night 21/22nd.

ACKNOWLEDGE.

19th JUNE 1916.

                                           A.K.McLeod Capt.
                                                Bde.Major.
Copies to;-   95th Inf.Bde.

5th Division.
15th Inf.Bde.
42nd Inf.Bde.
43rd Inf.Bde.
I/Devons.
I/E.Surreys
I/D.C.L.I.
12/Gloucesters.
1/6th A & S Highlanders.
1/2 Home Coun.Field Coy.R.E.
Browell's Group.
Bde.Signalling Officer.
95th Bde.M.G.Coy.
New Zealand.
O.C.TOBY Trench Mortar Bty.
95th Trench Mortar Battery.
No.3 Company Train.
S.O. 95th Inf.Bde.
Staff Capt.
Bde.Major.
Intelligence Officer.

Appendix VI

TRAINING PROGRAMME FOR WEEK ENDING - 24th INST.

6566666666666.66

	6-15 a.m.	8-30 a.m. - 12 Noon.	2-30 - 5 p.m.	TRAINING.
THURSDAY.	Physical Training.	D. Coy. To 5th Div. School, 8-30 a.m. to 9-30 a.m. A. Coy. & half B. Coy. 5th Div. School. 9-30 to 12-30 Half B, C & D. Coys. training from 9-30 a.m.	A. Coy. & Half B. Coy. 5th Div. School. Remainder. Coy. Training.	Tube Helmet Drill. Close Order Drill. Drill, Extended Order. Drill combined with Artillery formations and small schemes. Musketry to include Visual Training, Fire Orders, Firing positions, Tests, Instructions in care of arms and knowledge of rifle. Organization of Bombing Parties. Bayonet Fighting. PIONEER TRAINING. Instruction in revetting, rapid wiring, organization of working parties. Working on work and marking tasks.
FRIDAY.	DITTO.	C. Coy. to 5th Div. School, 8-30 a.m. to 9-30 a.m. A. Coy. & half B. Coy. as for Thursday. Half B, C & D. Coys. Training from 9-30 a.m.	As for Thursday.	

1. Working parties at 5th Div. School will draw tools as follows:- Complete Coy. from School Stores. These parties must report at the hour named at the School.
2. Shorts will only be worn by working parties and those authorized.
3. O.C. Coys. will render programmes of work showing hours and place where they are to be found, daily to Orderly Room by 9 a.m. And Lewis Detachment will invariably parade as strong as possible. Half Officers servants will attend
4. Coys. 8-30 a.m. parade.
5. Signallers and Lewis Detachment will keep the above hours and will render programmes as in para 3 O.C. Lewis Detachment will arrange to keep 51 N.C.Os and men always with the guns and will keep his reserve of 40 trained by turning them over with his regular detachment.
6. Company Scouts must be kept trained on a basis of 1 N.C.O and 12 men per coy.

(Sgd) A.G. Thomas, Captain,
Adjutant 1/6th. Bn. Arg. & Suth'd. Highrs.

21-6-16.

1/6th. Bn. Arg. & Suth'd. Highrs. No. S.2e/

appendix VII

SECRET.

1/6th. BATTN. ARG. & SUTH'D. HIGHRS.

O.C.

ORDERS FOR DUMPING SURPLUS STORES IN CASE OF AN EMERGENCY MOVE.

1. On receipt of these orders by Coys. etc. all surplus Officer's Kits and all surplus stores will be taken to the Battalion dump at *Chateau Stables, GRAND RULLECOURT, Reference Sheet 51c.010.c.3.1.*

2. 1 N.C.O. and 3 men, detailed by the Adjutant, will parade at Battn. Hqrs. in Marching Order, and will proceed to the Dump, where they will remain in charge until the stores are collected by the Corps. The Quartermaster will arrange to leave 14 days preserved rations with this party.

3. O.C. Coys., Officer's i/c Lewis Detachment, Signallers, Headquarter Details and Transport will render ~~duplicate~~ TRIPLICATE lists of stores dumped to the Orderly Room before departure of the Battalion. One copy will be given by the Adjutant to the N.C.O. i/c Dump. 2nd. Lieut. M.M. Muir will be responsible for the dumping of all surplus Quartermaster Stores and will render duplicate lists as above.

4. O.C. Coys. will each detail a party of 1 N.C.O. and 25 men to report to 2nd. Lieut. M.M. Muir at the Quartermaster Stores to carry stores to the Dump.

5. Captain, S. Coats will superintend the stacking of stores dumped.

6. Stores will be listed and dumped in the following categories :-

   (a) ORDANCE STORES INCLUDING
       Clothing and Quartermasters Stores,
       Latrine Buckets,
       Brooms,
       Syringes,
       Sayer Stoves,
       Baths,
       Washing basins,
       Blankets,
       Horse Rugs,
       Reserve Tube Helmets,
       Spare Harness and Transport Gear.

   (b) A.S.C. Stores.

   (c) R.E. Stores.
       All tools not held on charge under Mob. Store Tables.
       All material such as sandbags, wire, corrugated iron, timber, etc.

   (d) Medical Stores.

   (e) Veterinary Stores.

7. Officer's Kits, Canteen Stores and private property of the Battalion will be listed and stacked separately.

.... CAPTAIN
ADJT. 6TH ARG. & SUTHND HIGHRS

~~Lieut. Col.~~
~~Commanding 1/6th. Battn. Arg. & Suth'd. High~~

22-6-1?.

Appendix VIII

1/6th. Bn. Arg. & Suth'd. Highrs.

STATEMENT OF CASUALTIES, ADMISSIONS TO AND DISCHARGES FROM HOSPITAL.

WASTAGE.		REINFORCEMENTS.	
Killed.	-.	Fighting Strength, 31-5-16	779.
Wounded.	1.		
Missing.	-.	Returned from C.C.Stn.	5.
Sick evacuated to C.C. Stn. (Off Strength)	23.	TOTAL.	784.
Munition Workers.	6.		
Absentees.	2.		
Month's Leave.	2.		
Underage -To base.	1.		
Bde. M.G. Coy.	24.		
	59.		
Fighting Strength 30-6-16.	725.		
TOTAL.	784.		

30th June, 1916.

Captain,
Adjutant 1/6th. Bn. A. & S. H.

Appendix IX

LIST OF OFFICERS - 1/6th. Bn. ARG. & SUTH'D. HIGHRS.

Lieut. Col. R.I. Rawson.	Commanding Officer.
Major R.H.B. Haldane.	S
Captain. A.G. Thomas.	Adjutant.
Captain. S. Coats.	
Captain. H. McC. McHaffie.	
Captain. A. Craig.	
Captain. J.H. Brown.	
Captain. D.N. Robertson.	
Lieut. J.A.G. Shanks.	
Lieut. W. Shanks.	
Lieut. L.L. Shearer.	
Lieut. A. Lang.	
Lieut. C. Gardner.	
Lieut. J.H.E. Coats.	O.C. L.D.
Lieut. G.S. Nelson-Scott.	
Lieut. P. Harrington.	
Lieut. J.H. Stockdale.	
Lieut. R.C. Pollock.	
Lieut. D.A. Love.	
Lieut. C.W. Coats.	
2/Lieut. J.H.D. Hurst.	
2/Lieut. R.A. Brown.	
2/Lieut. J. Andrew.	
2/Lieut. W.H. McKilligan.	
2/Lieut. H.W. Whimster.	
2/Lieut. W.L. Smellie.	
2/Lieut. W.P. McCreath.	Hospital.
2/Lieut. J.W.L.T. McDonald.	
2/Lieut. M.M. Muir.	
2/Lieut. A. Shearer.	
2/Lieut. A. Nairn.	95th Bde. M.G. Coy.
2/Lieut. R.R. Waters.	
2/Lieut. J.W.R. Paine.	
2/Lieut. E. Orr.	
2/Lieut. A.G. Young.	Hospital.
2/Lieut. G.J. Pirie.	
2/Lieut. W. Muir.	
2/Lieut. J.D. Ramsey.	
2/Lieut. W.S. Muir.	
2/Lieut. A.L. Paterson.	
Lt. & Qr. Mr. Scaife, J.	
Captain. W.W. Phillips.	R.A.M.C.

www.ingramcontent.com/pod-product-compliance
Lightning Source LLC
Chambersburg PA
CBHW081359160426
43193CB00013B/2062